First printing: October 2023

Copyright © 2023 by Jenny Hubanks and Master Books®. All rights reserved. No part of this book may be reproduced, copied, broadcast, stored, or shared in any form whatsoever without written permission from the publisher, except in the case of brief quotations in articles and reviews. For information write:

Master Books, P.O. Box 726, Green Forest, AR 72638

Master Books® is a division of the New Leaf Publishing Group, LLC.

ISBN: 978-1-68344-296-7
ISBN: 978-1-61458-808-5 (digital)
Library of Congress Control Number: 2023946623

Cover: Diana Bogardus
Interior: Terry White

Images are from shutterstock.com.

Scripture quotations are from The ESV® Bible (The Holy Bible, English Standard Version®), copyright © 2001 by Crossway, a publishing ministry of Good News Publishers. Used by permission. All rights reserved.

Please consider requesting that a copy of this volume be purchased by your local library system.

Note that permission is granted for copies of reproducible pages from this text to be made for use with immediate family members living in the same household. However, no part of this book may be reproduced, copied, broadcast, stored, or shared in any form beyond this use. Permission for any other use of the material must be requested by email from the publisher at info@nlpg.com.

Printed in the United States of America

Please visit our website for other great titles:
www.masterbooks.com

For information regarding promotional opportunities, please contact the publicity department at pr@nlpg.com.

Table of Contents

Introduction 5
Chapter 1: A Positive Environment 7
Chapter 2: Visual Schedules 23
Chapter 3: Visual Supports 45
Chapter 4: Basic Learning Skills 61
Chapter 5: Teaching Strategies 73
Conclusion 81
Glossary 83
Index 85
Endnotes 87
Datasheets & Manipulatives 89
    Supply/Equipment/Software List 90
    Datasheets & Manipulatives Table of Contents 91
    Tokens 93
    Datasheets 133
    Manipulatives 147
Posters 209

About the Author

Jenny Hubanks is a Board Certified Behavior Analyst® (BCBA®) and a licensed special education teacher. She obtained her undergraduate degrees from Sterling College and the University of Kansas. Later, she completed a Master's in Adaptive Special Education from the University of Kansas. To further enhance her expertise, Jenny completed her coursework from the Florida Institute of Technology, and obtained her certification from the Behavior Analyst Certification Board (BACB). During her time as a classroom teacher, she primarily worked with students who had significant cognitive disabilities. This experience proved instrumental in teaching her the value of positive reinforcement, consistency, and fostering peer relationships. Jenny has also served as a Lead BCBA® in Northwest Arkansas, gaining valuable clinical experience, and started a company called Maven Learning Innovations.

Jenny loves seeing individuals from all walks of life succeed. In her leisure time, she devotes herself to her family, which includes her husband and her two young sons. Being a mother to young boys has provided her with invaluable insights into teaching and learning in a home setting. The remainder of her free time is dedicated to pursuing a doctoral degree in performance leadership improvement.

Nurturing Every Child's Unique Abilities

This is a practical and comprehensive guide designed to support educators, parents, and caregivers in helping children with special needs thrive academically, socially, and emotionally. In these pages, you will discover a wealth of knowledge, instructional insights, and valuable tools to create inclusive and empowering learning environments.

Every child has been created by God with unique talents and abilities waiting to be unlocked, regardless of their challenges or differences. The journey to empowering children with special needs begins with understanding, compassion, and the right strategies. This book is a compass, offering practical advice, evidence-based methods, and the latest insights in special education.

To make the learning experience even more engaging and effective, this book includes perforated pages featuring datasheets, visual aids, and manipulatives that can be easily incorporated into your teaching practices. These resources are designed to be practical, adaptable, and ready to use, ensuring that you can implement strategies seamlessly.

What You'll Find In This Book

Tailored Approaches: Discover a diverse array of customized methods, including innovative assistive techniques, designed to cater to the unique needs of every child.

Positive Learning Atmosphere: Acquire practical and proven methods for fostering an effective and empowering learning environment that encourages growth and self-confidence.

Sensory-Friendly Practices: Explore the possibilities and tools that enhance the learning experience, making it comfortable, pleasant, and enriching.

Nurturing Vital Skills: Equip yourself with the strategies needed to nurture essential daily skills in children with special needs, helping them build a solid foundation for their future.

Ready-to-Use Tools: Benefit from perforated pages featuring datasheets, visual aids, and manipulatives, conveniently designed for immediate use. Tokens and icons can be laminated, cut out, and sorted for use with the ready-made worksheets in the back.

A Grateful Acknowledgment

With sincere thanks to Darlene Magsam. Your collaboration and creative contributions truly elevated this project.

THRIVE: Special Needs Strategies That WORK!

For you formed my inward parts; you knitted me together in my mother's womb. I praise you, for I am fearfully and wonderfully made. Wonderful are your works; my soul knows it very well.

— Psalm 139:13-14

God made us each in His image with unique gifts and abilities. Many gifts and abilities are overlooked in today's society, but rest assured, our gifts were not given accidentally. We each have a purpose in God's kingdom. As a teacher, I had the privilege of helping children find their strengths and gifts and then teaching them how to use them. As a parent or educator, you have the same privilege. What an honor!

As I write this, I reflect on my years in the classroom; one of my top goals for each student was to teach them to be as independent as possible. I have spent most of my adult life working with children that have special needs in some capacity. My mission has always been to find the best strategies and tools to meet each individual's needs. The world of education is ever-changing, but some tried-and-true strategies give children with special needs better opportunities to learn new skills. Many of the strategies and tools in this book will apply to schoolwork and learning valuable life skills that will support independence throughout life.

The independence level of one child may not be the same as their sibling, cousins, or peers. Each child will learn independence skills at different rates. However, one thing all children have in common is the need to become more independent as they move through adolescence. Our job as a parent involves teaching our children many, many things. Continually teaching them to become more independent is one of the critical areas of focus. Essentially, we are working ourselves out of a job! Excuse me while I get a tissue just thinking about my boys moving out one day!

This book was written specifically for those teaching children with special needs, but these strategies can support all children regardless of diagnosis. My desire to create this book was to give educators resources to support a variety of challenges they face daily. This is not a one-size-fits-all book, but there are suggestions for modifying the strategies to different levels based on your child's needs.

Introduction

As you progress through the book, you may find that some children do not need all of the strategies, but one or more strategies will likely support them. You will also find that some strategies can be combined and will strengthen one another when used together.

As Andy Hargreaves said, "Change is easy to imagine, hard to implement, and incredibly difficult to sustain."[1] I have used these strategies and watched children blossom as they learn new skills and information with these supports, not only in a school setting but also at home. I have been using several strategies in this book with my children. It is not easy to make changes sometimes, but it is worth it!

As you work through this book, I encourage you to be patient. Some strategies will work quickly, while others need to be explicitly taught, and it can take longer to see the benefits of your hard work. Often it is easiest to make one change at a time, both for the adult and the child. Give yourself time to become familiar with the processes. Most importantly, I encourage you to give yourself grace while learning and implementing new things! Whether you are a seasoned teacher or this is a brand-new adventure, you can do this! The children will be blessed that you are taking on this challenge for them! I can't wait to begin this journey with you!

Using the Resources in the Back of This Book

❶ *Introduction to Figures and Teaching Resources:* You will notice the figures that correspond to the various strategies and teaching resources as you read through each chapter.

❷ *Location of Figures and Resources:* Many of these are provided in the back of the book in the Datasheets and Manipulatives section.

❸ *Identifying Available Resources:* You can see which ones were created for you by watching for this symbol next to the figure.

❹ *Purpose of Elements:* These elements often include the tokens that will be needed as you work through the information with your students.

❺ *Maintenance and Reusability:* Most of these sheets and tokens work best when laminated so they are sturdy and can be used more than once. The tokens can also have Velcro applied so that they can adhere to the appropriate spaces on the sheets.

❻ *Example of Figure 4.6:* See the example below of Figure 4.6, which is cleaning off the table. The sheet is available in the back, as well as the tokens that can be placed on it with Velcro adhesives.

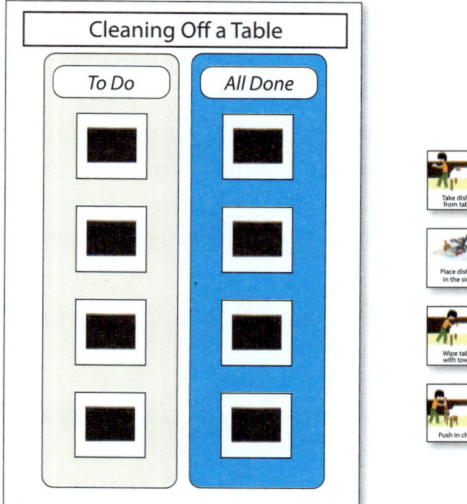

THRIVE: Special Needs Strategies That WORK!

A Positive Environment

Creating a positive working environment is one of the essential components of teaching. Take a moment to think back to your favorite school or Sunday school teacher. What characteristics do you recall about them? When I've asked this question in the past, responses typically fell into one or more categories described by the following: People fondly remember teachers who made them feel loved, safe, successful, independent, and valued, and they remember teachers that they thought believed in them. As an educator, many, if not all, of these characteristics will be something you already do!

One area that parents of children with special needs often ask me about is how to support their child in becoming more independent. Using positive reinforcement, we can take those significant characteristics listed above to help support independence.

A second key component to creating a positive working environment revolves around structure. When I started working from home during and after the pandemic, I had to create a work environment. As I prepared to set up my office space, I investigated what others used for a home office. I found a wide range of examples. I observed three main themes during my research.

1. The first was that the office did not need to be expensive to be functional.

2. My second observation was home offices were most often spaces dedicated to work. In other words, the area was structured to be conducive to completing work tasks.

3. Lastly, I noticed the area was organized for efficiency. Most people had items they needed right in their workspace.

As I reflected on these three main themes, I realized how similar these ideas are to a conducive learning environment for children. All humans desire positive and productive environments. For some adults and children, those come very naturally. For others, it will need to be explicitly taught. As a public school teacher, I typically used what furniture and materials were available. My first task as a self-contained teacher at the beginning of the school year was to structure the classroom to benefit my students. My next goal was to organize materials to be easily accessible and in the needed areas. These beginning components set the stage for learning.

Motivating Children

Positive reinforcement happens when you provide children with a reinforcer (an item THEY desire) after each child gives the response YOU want. If that response continues or is maintained, that item is currently reinforcing to the child and positive reinforcement is taking place.[2] Most of us do this naturally throughout the day. Reinforcers can be any item, food, social interaction, or activity. If a child finds it motivating and the item or activity is appropriate, you can use it as a reinforcer. Below, you will find a list of examples to get you started.

Potential reinforcers (items listed can often overlap categories):

Items/Objects	Toys	iPad/computer	Bubbles	Pet	Noise maker	Fan	Slime	Light-up toys
Food	Candy	Fruit	Juice	Popcorn	Chips	Peanut butter	Cereal	Pudding
Social	High five	Tickles	Fist bump	Verbal praise	1:1 time with adult	Hugs	Phone call	Cheering
Activity	Water play	Fingerpaint	Games	Shaving cream play	Bike ride	Go for a walk	Pretend play	Swing

THRIVE: Special Needs Strategies That WORK!

Often, educators will need no help coming up with ideas. They know exactly what a child desires. Other times, you might have difficulty finding items that a child likes. In that case, I encourage you not to give up! Here are some tips for finding potential reinforcers:

- Keep introducing new potential reinforcers. Don't give up!
- Introduce potential reinforcers multiple times. You never know when something will grab their interest.
- If you run out of ideas, do some research. There are many websites with potential ideas.
- Think outside the box. Sometimes children like things adults wouldn't expect.
- Watch them when they have free time. What are they doing when they look happy and engaged? That is your item or activity!

Now that we have laid the basic groundwork of positive reinforcement, you might be asking yourself, "Why should I use this?" We should use positive reinforcement to teach, increase, or maintain a skill or behavior. When adults ask why I recommend using positive reinforcement with children, I always ask the same question, "Would you continue going to work if your boss told you that you would no longer receive a paycheck?" Of course, the answer is always no! If you go to work and do your job, you get paid for your time. If you continue going to work to keep getting paid, that paycheck is positive reinforcement for you. I like to suggest teachers and parents think of school as our children's job. We expect them to go all day and complete specified tasks. It sounds like a job to me!

The following section will go through a few key components to brush up on when preparing to implement positive reinforcement. You probably do many of these things already.

1. Make items special.

The first task is gathering the items a child likes. You will want to have more than one item if a child becomes tired of something they choose multiple times. It is good to have items across various categories (food, activities, objects, social). Once you have those items, you want to ensure that a child does not have unlimited access to them throughout the day. You want these items to be special! If the items are only available during "work" times, they will be more powerful. It is also wise to rotate objects so that children do not become uninterested in some items by seeing them repeatedly. If a child only likes one or two objects, swapping in new things and providing access to them multiple times is a great way to allow them to explore new possibilities.

A Positive Environment

2. Follow through every time.

When you tell a child they can earn a motivating item for completing a task, it should hold the same weight as a promise. It is so crucial that you follow through with the deal you make. Kids figure out adults quickly and will remember if you do not follow through with your end of the agreement. Completing your end of the deal helps build trust and a positive working environment. A vital piece of being a person that always follows through is to only promise an item if you have access to it in the moment. It is also essential that you provide the reinforcer as soon as possible when they finish their task so its arrival will strengthen the desired behavior.[3] I always instructed my paraprofessionals and behavior technicians to get the item to the child within three seconds. The faster you provide their reinforcer, the more likely they will connect completing a task and getting a motivating thing. When adults consistently provide reinforcement, children learn if they do _____, they earn _____. This is an essential skill. To put it another way, it helps teach them cause and effect.

3. Neutral is necessary.

If you are a parent, you know that when you begin to implement new procedures with your child, they will not always be happy with the changes. I always told the other adults working in my room to try not to take the student's behavior personally in the classroom setting. When children have undesired behaviors, their goal is typically not to ruin the day of the adult they are near; the adults are collateral damage. Often, children with special needs have difficulty communicating, difficulty with change, emotional regulation challenges, and the list goes on.

In my experience, it is much more difficult as a parent not to take challenging behavior personally than it is as a professional. We work so hard to raise our children to the best of our ability, and it sure does feel personal when their behavior isn't what we desire. Take heart! Take a deep breath or any other strategy that works for you and give yourself time to think. Remind yourself, "This isn't personal." Do not try to reason or barter with children while in that intense emotional state. Let them calm down, then move forward. An additional piece of advice I gave adults in my classroom was to have a neutral or pleasant tone of voice and facial expression when working with a child. Even when things are tough, if your voice level rises or your face looks angry, it will likely escalate a child that is already feeling out of control. These slight shifts can make a big difference.

THRIVE: Special Needs Strategies That WORK!

How to Provide Positive Reinforcement

Now to the fun part! How do you use positive reinforcement during a child's learning time? I will describe the process and add some tips that I have learned along the way. For many kids, you may need to begin with a type of visual support. We will dive into different types of visual schedules in Chapter 2 and various visual supports in Chapter 3. Until then, keep the general term "visual support" as a placeholder for the specific types we will discuss in future chapters.

Process

- Have your visual support ready. Ask a child what they are working toward.
- State the instruction in short, simple terms.
- The child completes the task.
- Immediately hand them the item they chose to work for or a token. Remember to pair the token or item with praise telling them precisely what they did right.

Voila! You are on your way to positive reinforcement. The key to knowing if something truly is positive reinforcement is data. If you complete paper-based activities, you will have data from that source. However, if a child is working on hands-on tasks, I have included a datasheet in the back of this book to use or adapt to fit your needs. This data will allow you to see if your strategies are successful and will support making data-based decisions. After reviewing your data, if the desired behavior (the task you want the child to complete) continues to be completed or increases, you have achieved positive reinforcement success!

Figure 1.1. This datasheet can be used for many types of skills. The scoring code can be marked as you wish, just note your code at the top. I recommend using a new sheet for each skill so your data does not get mixed.

Now that you've seen the basic process, let's look at an example. This example assumes the child is seated in their work area.

- Present the child with a choice board for reinforcer selection. What are you working for (extend the visual toward the child so they can select an item)? When the child makes a selection, move to the next step.
- Present your demand (the task). For example, "Cut out the square."
- Make sure the child completes the task you requested.
- Immediately provide verbal praise ("You stayed so close to the lines, awesome!") and hand them the item or a token.
  - Specific: "close to the lines"
  - Praise: "awesome"
  - Concise: extra language was avoided
  - Quick delivery

A Positive Environment

1:1 Reinforcement

1:1 reinforcement is defined as having a child do one task, then providing them with one item or activity for reinforcement. If your child needs to start with 1:1 reinforcement, keep their breaks short if they choose an activity or item as a reinforcement. If they prefer an edible item, such as a gummy candy, they can eat the item and you can get back to work. Give 1–2 minutes at the most when giving them a break after every single task. Once they understand the concept of working to gain an item, you can increase them to completing two tasks for a reinforcer, and so on. When I add another task, I ask the child to do something that I know they can do quickly and easily so they see it is still the same promise. Once they complete more tasks (and take more time), you will increase the amount of time they get for a break.

I typically stick with a 5-minute reinforcement break at the most. It all depends on how much work they completed. The process of extending to working longer can take time, depending on your child, but it is well worth it. Some children will need a visual to support this learning. If your child has difficulty moving beyond doing one task and then getting one item, this next section is for you.

Token Boards

Some children will need to start with 1:1 reinforcement. Others will be able to do multiple tasks before receiving a reinforcement break. A token economy is another way to implement positive reinforcement. A specified number of tokens are earned and traded for a reinforcer.[4] A token board is a type of token economy and can have varying styles. I have seen token boards begin with one token and build up to 25. After that, the sky is the limit! I am providing some examples of token boards. If your child loves specific toys (e.g., cars, figures), you can buy token boards with specific designs by searching for the item and "token board" online. You will notice there are many options.

Figure 1.2. Token boards can be created in Google Slides or another computer program. Once they are printed (I suggest cardstock), you can laminate the page and cut out the tokens. Placing Velcro on the back allows the tokens to be used on the front and stored on the back.

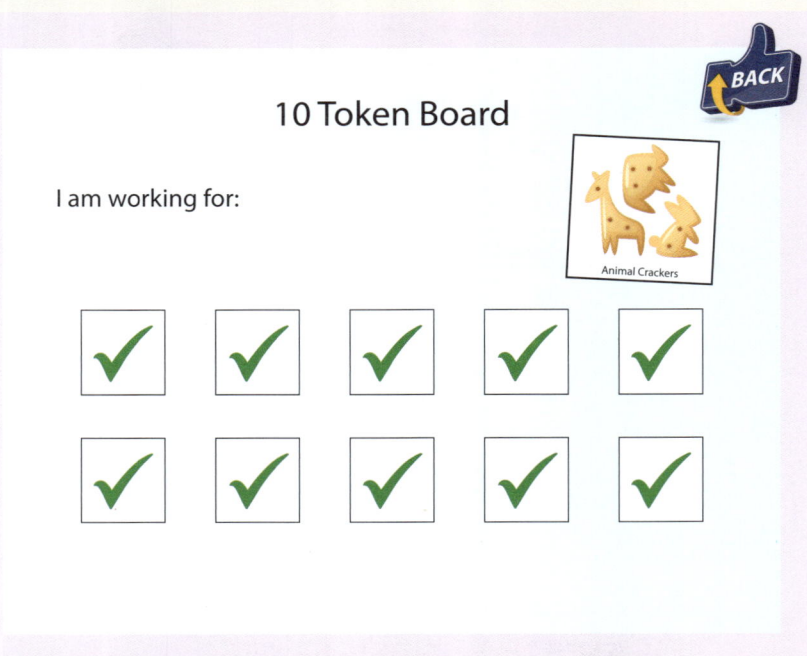

Figure 1.3. This token board was created from a coloring book. I colored the image, cut it out, and glued it to cardstock. I then cut it into four pieces, laminated it, and cut it out again. I also outlined the image on the other half of the cardstock and laminated it for a landing board. I then added Velcro to connect the top pieces and the bottom. You can use any picture to create this type of token board. In the past, I took character folders you buy before school starts and cut them to make boards. If you selected a favorite item, be prepared for your child to think they are only working for that item. However, an "I am working for" sentence at the bottom will provide space for them to select an item and remind them that there are other choices.

Figure 1.4. Token boards can be handwritten on a piece of paper. You can draw this anytime and anywhere you have paper and a writing utensil. In this example, the child's task is taking bites of their meal to earn ice cream. The behavior of taking bites is being reinforced with smiley faces until they reach the end goal of ice cream!

Figure 1.5. Token boards can be created on dry erase boards. They are erased and drawn again to reset.

Figure 1.6. This token board was created using an old DVD case. Construction paper was written on and added to the inner sleeve. Velcro was placed on the outside and pennies were added for tokens. This is a great way to practice learning money! (Tokens for this are provided in the back.)

A Positive Environment

Figure 1.7. Placing Velcro on the back of token boards provides a place for extra token storage and extra reinforcer icons!! (Tokens are in the back.)

Figure 1.8. This choice board has space for six reinforcer choices. It is made with Velcro, lamination, and labeled images from a program designed for creating icons. If more choices are needed, it could be made a full sheet.

Teaching Token Boards

If a child needs to start with 1:1 reinforcement, teach them to use a token board and strategically extend the number of tokens (and amount of work completed) they collect before each reinforcement break. Initially, to use a token board, you will need to pair the reinforcing item they choose to the tokens to help them understand that getting tokens equals getting their item. Small edible items such as a colorful treat work very well to aid in helping a child connect the token board to reinforcement. They eat their treat, and you are quickly ready to move forward. With a toy, you will have to go through getting the item back.

Choose the number of tokens you believe a child can successfully work toward to begin. I typically start children with five and extend to ten. For this example, we will start with five tokens. To teach a token board, you will begin with four tokens pre-loaded on the board. When the child completes the assigned task, you immediately deliver the token. This can happen in one of two ways. Some children will need the adult to place the token on the board, while others will be able to take the token and put it on themselves. Once the token is on, the adult will count the tokens from left to right (this reinforces pre-literacy skills). This might sound like, "One, two, three, four, five. You got the iPad. Way to go!" The child does not have to count the tokens. That is an extra task. Consider it a bonus if they do! Once they understand the concept of gaining a token, you will pre-load with three tokens, then two, then one, and finally, start with a blank token board. I suggest stopping at a ten-token board. Once they are in a groove with ten tokens, you can begin extending the number of tasks they do for each token (two tasks for one token and so on).

Removing Tokens

I do not recommend removing tokens. Earlier, we likened school to a child's job. I love the following example and have used it for a long time to explain this concept to adults because the message always rings true. Imagine you go to work one day, and you are five minutes late. Later in the day, you make a snappy comment to a coworker. When you clock out to leave, your boss notifies you that you are fined for those infractions. You were there ALL day. That's not right! Do you see where I'm going? Leave those tokens on until you reset. You might be thinking, "Well, what do I do if I hand them a token and they rip their paper?" Those things happen. When they do, I recommend reminding them what they chose to work toward. "You are working for the light spinner. You need two more tokens. Let's tape this paper." The first desired behavior you see, give them a token and tell them why.

A word of caution, though: kids will figure out loopholes in places we would never imagine them. I want to give you an example I often see to help illustrate how to best use the strategy I just suggested. In classrooms, teachers will generally want students to sit. One method often used is providing tokens for sitting. Usually, an adult is close enough to give the child a token after a designated number of seconds (and eventually minutes) of sitting. I have seen a loop that I want you to watch for so that you do not get stuck in it.

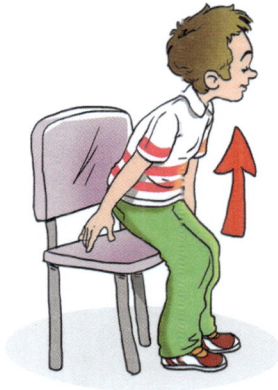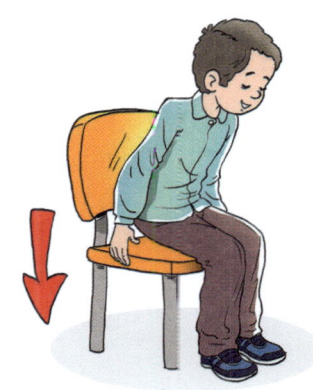

The student stands up.

The adult says, "Sit down."

The child sits down.

The adult says, "Great job sitting, here's a token."

This plays on a loop because the child has figured out if they stand up and then sit back down, they get a token. That's smart! What do I do instead? Let's look at a different way to use tokens for sitting.

The student stands up.

The adult says, "Sit down."

The child sits down.

The adult says, "Count to five. Touch your toes. You counted to five and touched your toes, AND you are sitting! Way to go! Here's a token."

This is just an example. Different behaviors than sitting could be exchanged, and the adult could assign other tasks, depending on the student's skills and as long as they are easy for the student to complete. The key is that the student has to engage in "work" before getting a token for sitting. This also often distracts them from the stand-up/sit-down game to get them involved in the activity.

A Positive Environment

Presenting Reinforcement Choices

Some children will need assistance in making choices regarding what they want to work toward, while others will tell you. Below are some visuals that can help a child make a selection. To use these visuals, you need pictures of the items a child likes. The number of things you present depends on how many visuals a child can scan, how many options you have available, and how many items you are willing to let them play with in that moment.

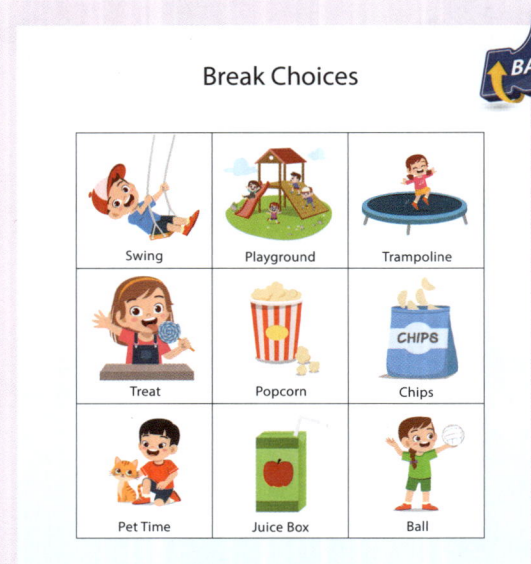

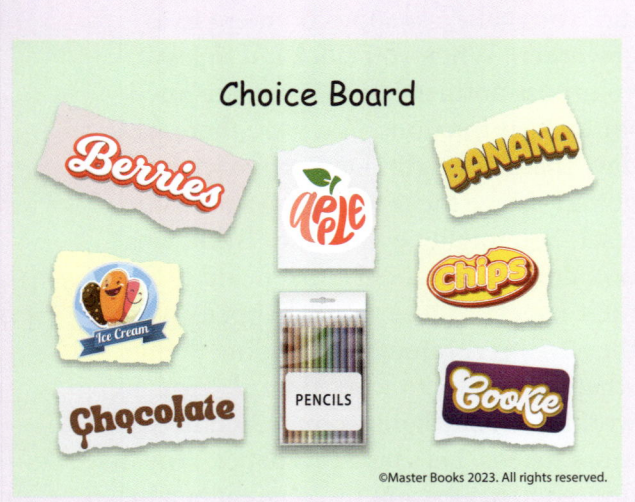

Figure 1.9. This choice board has printed choices on a piece of paper. The choices are not interchangeable and would need to be reprinted if something was not available on a particular day. Remember, do not offer it if it is not available!

Figure 1.10. This board was made from food/toy labels kept from shopping. Not only is it clever, but it is also an environmental print.

Figure 1.11. A clear container is another way to present potential reinforcers for selection if the child does not grab items and refuse to return them.

Pro tip: I want to share some pro tips and FAQs regarding positive reinforcement. There are often many questions about this topic. Hopefully, I can answer some of them for you before they come up.

Getting Reinforcing Items Back

Often, adults want to provide children with items they have earned, but they cannot get the items back when they do. It is always advised to warn children that their time is coming to an end. You can tell them verbally, use a visual timer, a timer sound, or a combination. Below, I explain how to use three similar methods to get items back from your child without challenging behaviors.

Open Hand Method

Reach your hand out toward the child with an open palm facing up.

Say, "Put in."

When the child places the item in your hand, immediately respond with, "Thank you for handing me your (item), you can have more time."

Set a new timer.

Repeat, adding in a delay on returning the item to the child.

As the child becomes faster at returning items, you can continue to increase the amount of time you keep the item (and they work). Be sure to throw in a surprise freebie every once in a while so they are always wondering when it will happen.

Container Method

The container method will often work for kids because it is like a neutral party. You aren't taking their item, they are just putting it in a container. I recommend placing the container where they can see it but not reach it. I recommend a clear container. While not necessary, it allows your child to see the item so they know it is still there waiting on them to complete their task.

Hold a clear container (large enough to hold their reinforcing item) out toward the child.

Say, "Put in."

Continue with the same process as the open hand method above.

A Positive Environment

Promise Procedure

If a child is very resistant to returning items, this is a great strategy to use to begin teaching them how to return an item. This procedure can be used with the open hand or container method.

Hold up an item the child likes (small edible item recommended) where the child can see it but not reach it.

Reach the other hand out, palm up, toward the child (or hold a container).

Say, "Put in."

As soon as the child places the item in your hand or the container, hand the edible item to them as you pull back your hand/the container holding the reinforcing item.

As the child becomes quick to return items, begin reducing the size of the edible item until you fade it out completely.

What If the Process is Still Not Working?

Stop and assess. Where is the process falling apart? Is it at the beginning? Check the task you requested them to complete and consider if it is too hard or too much work for the size or amount of the reinforcer. Make sure you have reinforcers the child really wants to earn.

Are you having difficulty at the end? In that case, I recommend you slow down the process. Spend more time immediately giving them back the item until they are comfortable knowing you will give them the item back. Once they know you will give it back when you say, this process becomes much easier! I do not recommend taking the item from them. When you take an item, they are less likely to think you will ever give it back.

 **Pro tip:** For getting back iPads/iPhones: Set guided access with a timer if you have a hard time getting your child off of the iPad or iPhone when their timer goes off. You can find many tutorials using a search engine. It is a quick and drama-free way to end your child's electronics time and keep them in the apps they can use.

Additional Tips

- *Be mentally present.* Make it fun — interact with children during their free time. Play with them! However, keep questions at a minimum; children can see questions as demands. If a child is hesitant to let you touch their toy, don't push it. You want the time to be enjoyable to them. You can slowly build up engaging with items.

- *Give the child choices.* Let them choose what they want to work toward each time. Do not assume you know. If something is unavailable, offer controlled choices. Controlled choices would include items that you do have available or are willing to let them select while still allowing the child to make the selection.

- *Make sure you pair the token with verbal praise.* We eventually want to use praise as reinforcement for a child. Some children need to have verbal praise paired with their favorite items over time so the verbal praise becomes valuable too. Smile — give high fives, fist bumps, and hugs too.

- *Examples of verbal praise:* "Awesome job writing your answer!" "Thank you for sitting in your seat while you work!" "Super job counting; here's a token!"

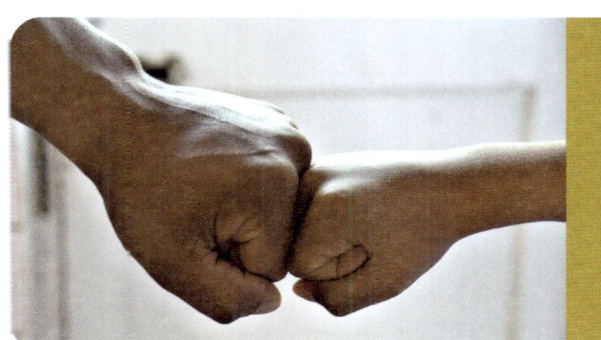

- *When you give directions, be clear, concise, and to the point.* As adults, we often add more language than necessary to get our point across. Some children with special needs stop attending after 2–3 words. Keep it short and simple.

- *Get items ready.* If your child often chooses iPad games, videos, or other electronic games, get the item ready while they complete their task. You want to make sure they can access the item immediately when they are finished.

- *Storing Tokens.* Store extra tokens on the back of token boards with Velcro.

FAQs for Positive Reinforcement

- *What if they stop working?*

The first thing I would look at is the amount of work presented for their chosen item. Is it too much work for the item? The amount of work needs to match the reinforcer. For example, if the child decides to work for one Skittle® and is given ten tasks to complete, that one Skittle® might not be enough. Some children may not find a Skittle® "worth it" for ten tasks. The second thing I would check is to see if they like any of their item choices enough to work for them. Even if they love an item, they can get tired of it for a while. For example, I love chocolate-covered toffee, but I might choose to work for something else after two or three pieces. The next day I might be interested in my chocolate-covered toffee again, or maybe I will have moved on to popcorn.

- *What if they refuse to choose an item?*

Again, I would make sure there are enough choices available that they find appealing. It might be that you need to rotate in some other options. If you get something they want enough, they will make a choice.

A Positive Environment

⊙ *What if they choose an item to work toward and then refuse to complete the task after I present it?*

Again, we want to make sure the task matches the reinforcer. Let them have a different reinforcer choice if they desire and see if that makes a difference. If not, consider the amount of work you are presenting and break it into chunks.

⊙ *What if I give them their earned item and they do not want it anymore?*

It is okay for kids to change their minds. We all change our minds sometimes. Make sure to set a timer and show them so they know even if they switch toys, the amount of time stays the same.

⊙ *What if I can't get a child to give the toy back, etc.?*

Reread the section from before on getting reinforcing items back.

⊙ *What if a child can't manipulate Velcro for a choice board?*

No problem! Not all children need a choice board. You can use a plastic bin that holds their options. They can select from the container, and you can place the item at the top of the table where the child can't reach it but can see it while they work.

⊙ *What if a child doesn't seem to care about positive reinforcement and still engages in challenging behavior?*

Some children value adult attention above all other things or prefer their items with adult attention. If a child likes adult attention more than items or wants you to engage with them while they have their items, you will need to ensure that you are providing high-quality attention. When we are in the high-quality attention zone, we want to focus entirely on the child. Cell phones and electronics are unavailable. We are not working on anything else. Kids know when we are pretending to be engaged. If children do not get the positive attention they want, they will settle for negative attention. If that is your child, lay the positive attention on thick.

If you continue to follow the positive reinforcement steps and find that things are not going as you expected, use this checklist to track your efforts next time. Sometimes even when we know how to do something, we forget a step. This is a quick and easy tool to help troubleshoot issues.

Figure 1.12. This checklist can be used to ensure that all of the steps necessary for successfully using positive reinforcement are in place.

Positive Reinforcement Checklist

1	☐ Let the child choose the item they are working toward (verbal, gesture, visual). Troubleshooting: Are they genuinely interested in any of the items at this moment in time?
2	☐ Present your demand. Troubleshooting: Use a neutral or pleasant voice and facial expression.
3	☐ Give the child adequate time to complete the task. Troubleshooting: Remind them what they chose to work toward if stalled.
4	☐ Present the child with the reinforcer they selected. Troubleshooting: Was the item delivered within three seconds?
5	☐ Set a timer to signal the end of reinforcement time. Troubleshooting: Does the child need to see a visual timer, or will a verbal reminder do?

Fidgets

The term "fidgets" can mean many different items. Any quick internet search using the term "fidgets" will bring up a plethora of options. Common examples of fidgets include chair bands, spinners, tangle toys, squishy balls, gum, and pop-its. However, a fidget can be anything that a person uses to engage in motor movements while at the same time engaging in their current activity. In my opinion, the best fidgets can be held in one hand. If there are other learners in the same area, fidgets should be quiet so others are not disturbed. Finally, you must teach the use of fidgets. Children should know that they are supporting tools, not toys. If they become distracting and are not being used appropriately, they should take a break and try again in the future. Not every type of fidget will be appropriate for every learner, so be sure to try different types of fidgets.

Structuring the Learning Environment

Creating a structured learning environment is essential for many children with special needs. Providing structure allows them to have a predictable and consistent environment, which is vital for children. Within the design of your learning setup, some children will need additional visual boundaries to organize and support their day. The space for a child will depend on their specific needs and skill level, but you can adapt the suggestions in this section to provide varying levels of support. Structure doesn't have to be boring. Make it fun! Let a child help choose and create what they can.

If teaching in a home, and you have access to a room in the home that is not used daily, that is a great place to set up for teaching and learning. If you have a room in the home to dedicate to education, that allows a child to have a visual change when it is time for school. For some children, this can be very important. They need that visual cue that it is no longer free time.

As you create your learning environment, many families use areas currently in use for other living activities due to space constraints. That is absolutely acceptable. Use what you have! There are ways to add items to change the environment so that children see a visual cue that it is time for school. For example, you can have a child pick out a special pillow to sit on or a particular "school time" lamp for the table. Be creative when designing your spot. You want the items to visually say, "It's school time," to a child. Another idea is to have them decorate a tri-fold poster board that you pull out for school like the one on the next page.

A Positive Environment

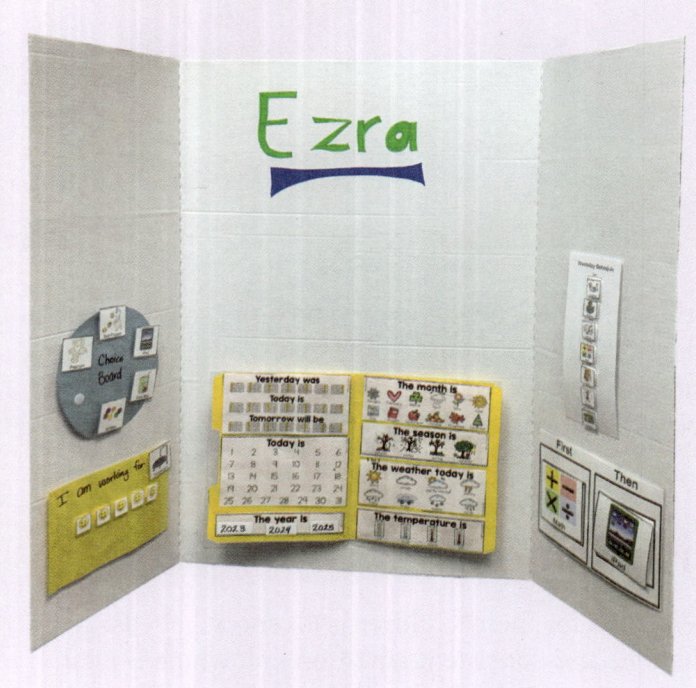

Figure 1.13. A workspace barrier can be created from a tri-fold poster board. It could include as many or as few accessories as desired. This example has a schedule, token board, choice wheel, first/then board, and a morning meeting visual.

Remember to keep your space simple. The more items included, the more opportunities for distraction. As a teacher, I kept a three-tier plastic rolling cart at each student desk to store any items I needed for each child so their work area remained clutter-free. If you find yourself removing items often, try a cart for supplies and see if it helps. The three-tier rolling cart was a tremendous support to me as a teacher. You want to ensure that you have all the needed supplies when you sit down. I could store task supplies, reinforcers, token boards, timers, crayons, and many other items right next to me. Wait time is hard for many people, especially children with special needs. Have everything ready to go! In Chapter 3, we will review specific visual boundary strategies that can support the learning environment.

WRAP-UP

If you are struggling with having your child complete tasks, you can begin this process today! Begin with positive reinforcement, structure the workspace, and get organized. These seem like small steps, but they make a huge difference and set the stage for success. In Chapters 2 and 3, we will discuss other ways to structure a child's day with visual schedules and visual supports.

> The steadfast love of the Lord never ceases;
> his mercies never come to an end;
> they are new every morning;
> great is your faithfulness.
> —Lamentations 3:22-23

2 Visual Schedules

Imagine you have the task of keeping all daily appointments, activities, and events for your family organized in your head. For this task, you only have access to your memory to ensure that everyone in your family makes it to all events on time. I can imagine that those with memory as a strength will be able to succeed in that endeavor. For the rest of us, that would prove to be a daunting task.

Adults have access to unlimited resources to help organize their lives. We use our phones to set ourselves reminders. We schedule our days, weeks, and months out on digital and paper calendars. We fill out planners and leave sticky notes to ensure we remember to do the thing we can't forget! Shouldn't we provide that level of structure and support to our children? Yes, we should!

Visual schedules are a type of visual support that provide structure and help a child navigate their day. They are detailed and fully customizable, allowing each child to have a visual schedule that fits their current developmental level. When taught to use visual schedules, children can learn valuable life skills.

Parents and teachers get excited when they learn visual schedules are an excellent strategy for decreasing challenging behavior and increasing independence. They should! In elementary and middle school, visual supports such as schedules have proven effective in reducing transition time, increasing on-task behavior, and completing self-help in the home.[5] Visual schedules can help children learn to sequence and organize their day.[6] As with many adults, some children will feel a sense of accomplishment as they check off tasks throughout their day. When additional teaching strategies are employed, visual supports can also support a child when learning to accept change and use self-management strategies.

You might be asking yourself, "Does a child need a visual schedule?" Ask the following questions with this child in mind.

- Does a child become frustrated during a typical school day?

- Does a child show signs of anxiety during a typical school day?

- Does a child need frequent or constant support to be successful with school?

- Does a child have a difficult time understanding directions presented verbally?

If the answer to any of these questions is yes, research indicates that the child would likely benefit from a visual schedule.[7]

In this chapter, we will dive into the many types of visual schedules. We will discuss selecting one that is just right for the child and teaching them to use it successfully. There are customization examples in each section to help give you ideas as you prepare to create a visual schedule for the child. I also throw in some tips and tricks that I learned along my journey. Let's get started!

Visual Schedule Types

There are several options to consider when selecting a visual schedule for a child. We will review several variations of visual schedules and some key details that will help determine if that type of schedule is a good selection. The following schedule types begin with the most intensive and progress to the least. The suggestions are a guide educators should consider, along with the information they know about a child. If you try a schedule type and find it unsuccessful, use the information gathered from the trial to inform your next attempt. Then, keep trying until you find the right fit! It is also a great idea to take a child's preference into account. If you are concerned they will choose a type that is not on their learning level, give them controlled choices. When giving controlled choices, you present two or three options to a child that you are willing to accept. Giving choices allows the child to feel a sense of control while allowing the adult to control the outcome.

The end goal is for the child to use the visual schedule as independently as possible. After the teaching component, we want them to use their visual schedules without our help. Since independence is our goal, it is essential to select a visual schedule that will allow the adult to systematically fade support. I recommend combing through all of Chapter 2 before making a selection.

You can present a visual schedule in a left-to-right or top-to-bottom format. After selecting the presentation style, you will need to determine how many items to present at a time. If a child does not sequence, you should begin with one item displayed on the schedule.[8] Then, when the child attends to one item and transitions without difficulty, add a second and build up to the total number of possible items on your selected format.

Pro tip: If in doubt, use a schedule! It is better to have the structure available and the child not need it.

Object Schedule

Object schedules are the most distinctive type of visual schedule. When creating an object schedule, you will need to select objects representing activities or locations the child will need throughout their day. If a child already associates an object with an activity or location, use it!

Figure 2.1. Object schedules can be created on hard, portable surfaces such as a clipboard. Items should attach to be removable so the child can take it with them to their next location.

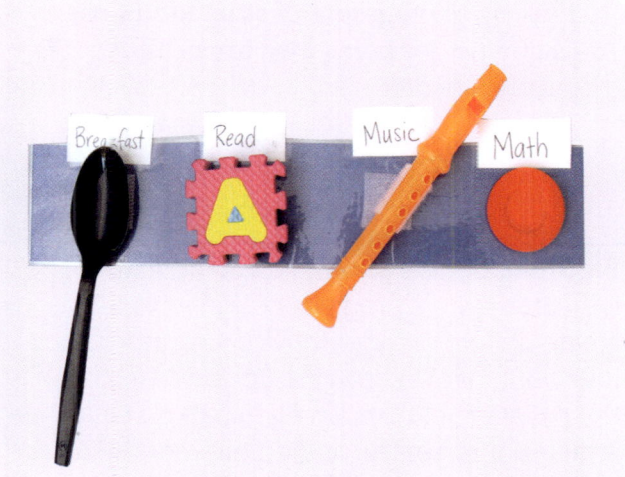

Figure 2.2. This object schedule was created using construction paper, Velcro, tape, and objects that represent activities.

Figure 2.3. This object schedule was created for a visually impaired child using objects and items with different textures attached to foam pieces. The foam is attached to laminated construction paper and can be pulled off and transported to other locations.

Object schedule selection considerations: Object schedules are beneficial for children not yet communicating with words or signs. Many times these children will communicate with gestures and objects. If a child's current communication style does not have shared meaning with others (do you find yourself guessing?), object schedules are an excellent place to start! They are also suitable for children with visual impairments.

Transitioning to a new schedule style: When a child attends to their schedule objects and transitions without challenging behavior or adult support, you can begin the transition process. Start by pairing each object with a photograph that will replace the object. Once a child begins to attend to the photograph, you then fade out the object.

Variations: The way object schedules are presented vary based on how you decide to create the layout. Above you will see several variations. I hope that seeing different options will allow you to explore features that could benefit a child. It is always acceptable to use what you already have around your house if you have something that works.

Photograph Schedules

Photograph schedules are created by taking photographs of exact locations, activities, or items used for a child's daily schedule.

Figure 2.4. This photograph schedule shows photographs that have been labeled and laminated. Velcro connects the cards to a laminated piece of construction paper, allowing for transportation to other locations.

Figure 2.5. This photograph schedule is created from a program designed to create uniform images for visual supports. Photographs are captured, uploaded into the program, printed, and laminated. Velcro attaches them in the desired order of the day to a laminated schedule page.

Figure 2.6. This photograph schedule is created from a program designed to create uniform images for visual supports. Photographs are captured, uploaded into the program, printed, and laminated. The child then checks off each activity as they work through the day with a dry-erase marker.

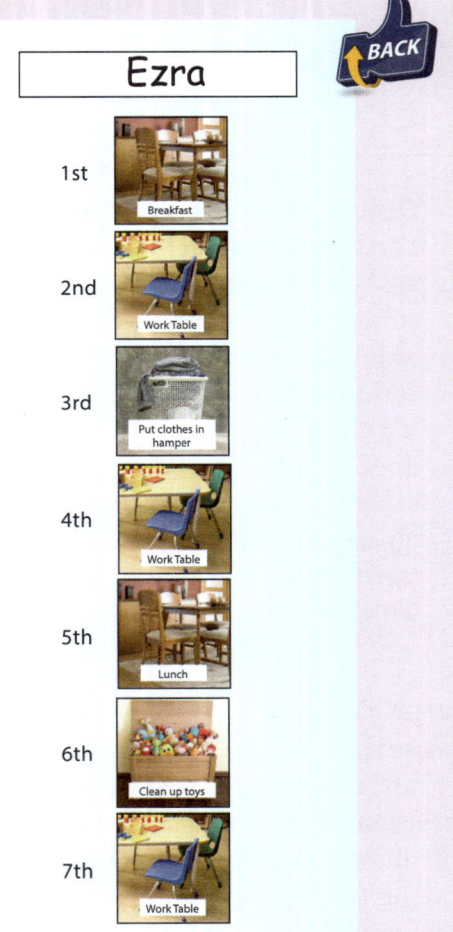

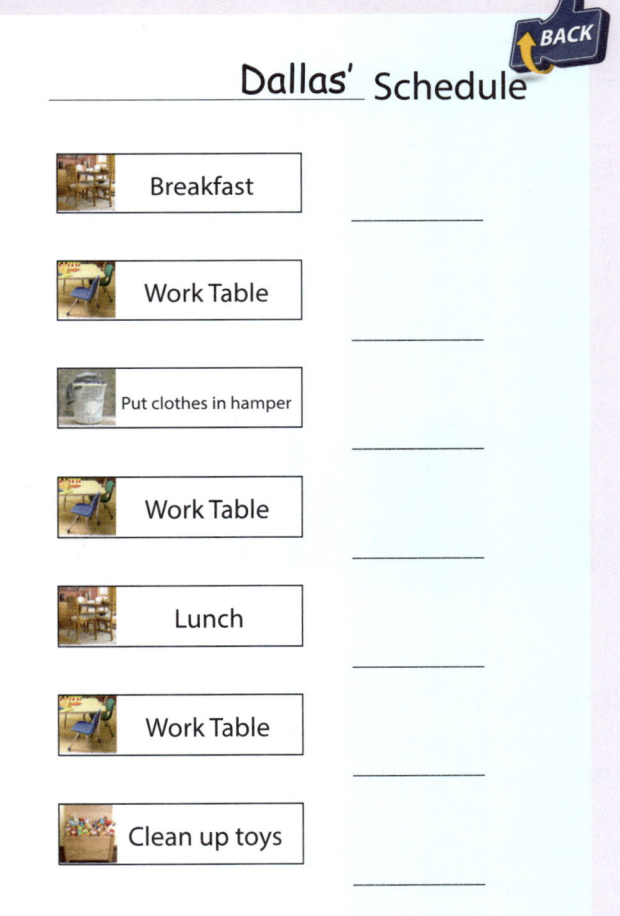

THRIVE: Special Needs Strategies That WORK!

Photograph schedule selection considerations: If a child understands pictures represent actual items and places, you are ready for a photograph visual schedule.[9] Photograph schedules are a great place to begin when a child cannot yet look at a drawing or cartoon image of a location or item and match it to their daily surroundings.

Transitioning to a new schedule style: When a child begins to transition to the location shown on their photograph schedule without challenging behavior or adult support, you are ready to transition to an icon schedule. Start by pairing the photographs with icons that will transition into the photograph's place. Once a child attends to the icon, you will begin to fade out the photographs. You can begin to fade out photographs by creating smaller ones, so they begin to shrink. Another option would be to put the icon on top of the photographs.

Variations: Photographs can be used to make different types of schedules. Determining how a child's schedule looks will depend on the child's skills and needs. Several variations are presented on the previous page for consideration, but this is not an exhaustive list. Feel free to be creative using the information in this chapter.

Icon Schedules

You create an icon schedule using images that represent activities, items, and locations that a child needs to navigate through the day. Often these images are created by a purchased program, but it is not necessary. Other options include drawing images or using a search engine to locate free images.

Figure 2.7. This icon schedule is from a program designed to create uniform images for visual supports. Each image has a label. The icons are glued onto construction paper. A check box has been created using Velcro. The child closes the tab after each activity to signal it is completed.

Figure 2.8. The distinction in this image from the previous one is that there is not a completion tab to close. Using this type, the child would return the icon to the designated area. These types of icon schedules sometimes need to be re-loaded throughout the day.

Figure 2.9. This icon schedule is from a program designed to create uniform images for visual supports. The icons remain on the page and are laminated. As the child completes an activity, they check off each activity with a dry-erase maker. Another option is to print it daily and let the child check it off with a writing utensil.

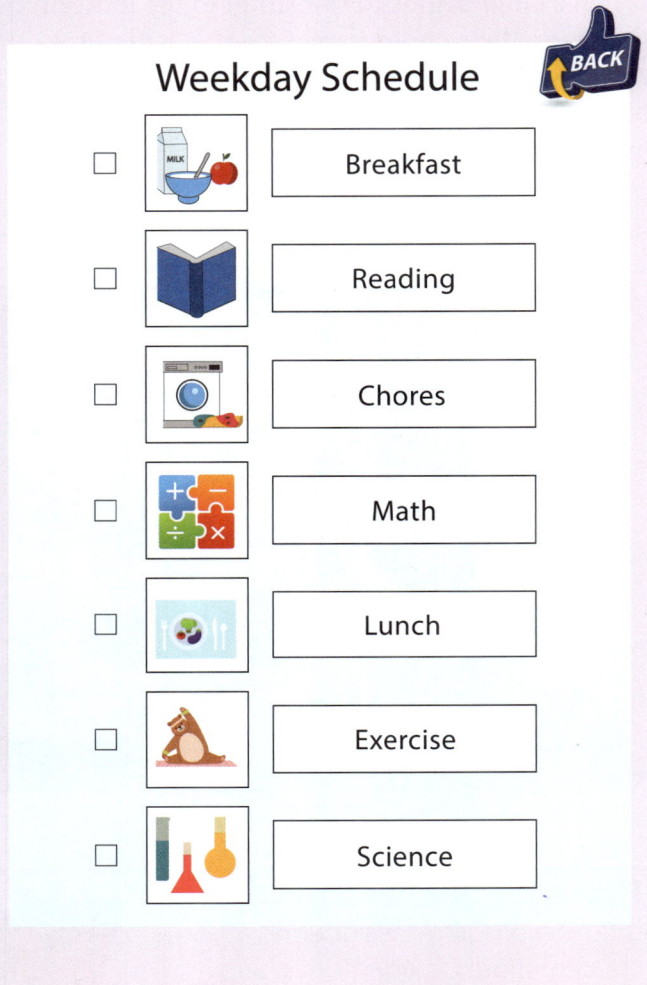

…they who wait for the Lord shall renew their strength;
they shall mount up with wings like eagles;
they shall run and not be weary;
they shall walk and not faint.

—Isaiah 40:31

Figure 2.10. This icon schedule is made using a program designed to create uniform images for visual supports. Icons are attached to a laminated sheet with Velcro. As the child completes activities, they move the icon over to the finished column. This schedule could need to be re-loaded throughout the day, or multiple pages could be created and loaded in order inside the binder.

Icon schedule selection considerations:
Icon schedules are a great place to begin when a child can look at a cartoon image of a location or item and match it to their daily surroundings. For example, a child who can look at three different cartoon images or drawings of a horse and understand each picture represents a horse is likely ready for icon schedules.

Transitioning to a new schedule style:
When a child begins to transition to the location shown on their icon schedule without difficulty, start reducing the icons' size and make the labels more prominent. You can start to fade out icons by creating smaller ones, so the image reduces in size, and the text takes the main focus.

Variations:
As with the other styles, icon schedules have many design options. I added some of my favorite variations on the previous pages to inspire you as you make a selection for the child.

Digital programs for icons:
There are several programs available for purchase at varying price points if you would like uniform icons.

You can also find apps that are cost-effective and completely customizable, with many unique features for those who prefer a digital schedule on an iPad or iPhone.

In times of patience and waiting, remember the beautiful promise of Isaiah 40:31. These words remind us that as we trust in God's plans and purpose and patiently endure life's challenges, our strength will be renewed. Just like eagles soaring, we will find ourselves capable of rising above adversity. When we persevere, we can run our race without growing weary and walk our path without fainting. This verse offers a profound message of hope, assuring us that our waiting will be rewarded with newfound strength and resilience. So, keep the faith, for in your patience, you are preparing to soar to new heights and overcome whatever comes your way.

Visual Schedules

Words with Icons Schedule

Words with icons schedules are created using images representing activities and locations that a child needs to navigate through the day. There is a slight distinction between the icon schedule mentioned previously and words with icons. In this style, the word becomes the main focus, and the icon takes a minor role.

There are cost-effective online icon options with various alternatives on the market. Many of these alternatives offer robust libraries, sizing options, and templates for a variety of activities and personalized learning games. Prices may vary, so it's a good idea to explore different options to find the one that suits your needs best.

Figure 2.11. This words with icons schedule is designed using a word processing program. Icons are inserted next to the words for clarity, but the words take more space on the schedule and are much more prominent. The child checks off each activity as they work through the day.

Figure 2.12. The words with icons schedule below is made using a program designed to create uniform images for visual supports. Icons are next to the words to assist understanding. There are Velcro check-off tabs the child closes when they complete the activity.

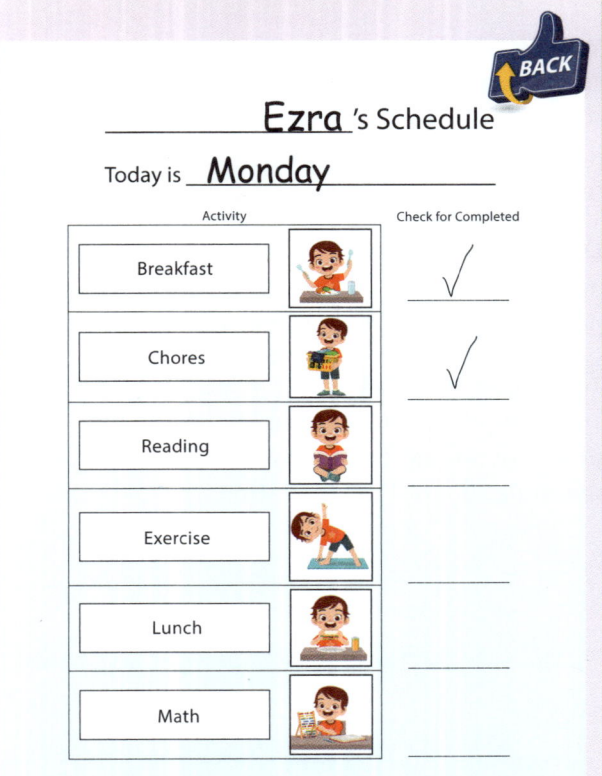

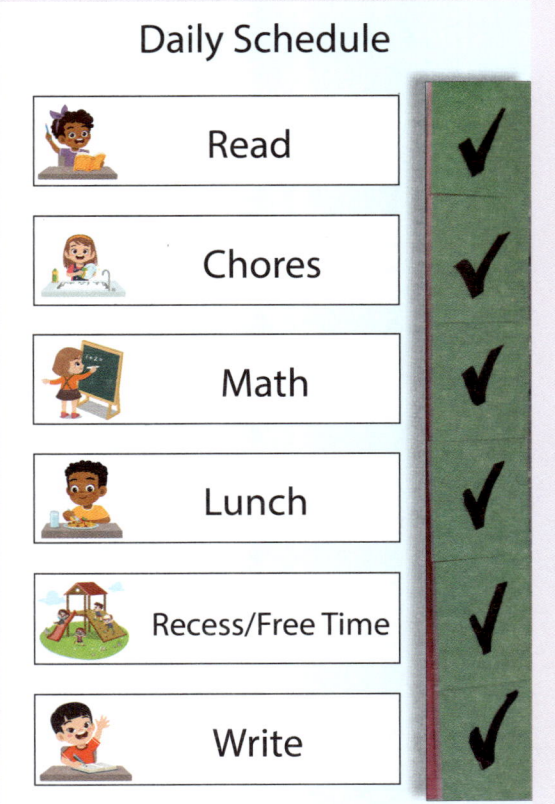

Transitioning to a new schedule style:
When a child begins to transition to the location shown on their words with icons schedule without support, start reducing the size of the icon even more. As the child begins to respond to the word, continue to slowly reduce the size until transitions are smooth without the need for the image.

Variations: As with the other schedule styles, words with icons schedules have multiple design options. Determining which presentation style to select will continue to depend on the child's skills and needs. The images on the next page provide some template ideas for this type of schedule but are by no means an exhaustive list.

THRIVE: Special Needs Strategies That WORK!

Words

A words-only schedule type is similar to using a student planner or calendar. They can be typed or hand-written. An adult can have the child help create the schedule for the day each morning, or they can be prepared in advance. Words-only schedules are a great way to teach children to organize their day. Creating a daily schedule is a strategy that a child could likely use all through their life.

Figure 2.13. This words-only schedule template is printed, laminated, and filled out with a dry-erase marker each day. It could also be used without lamination and a pen or other writing utensil.

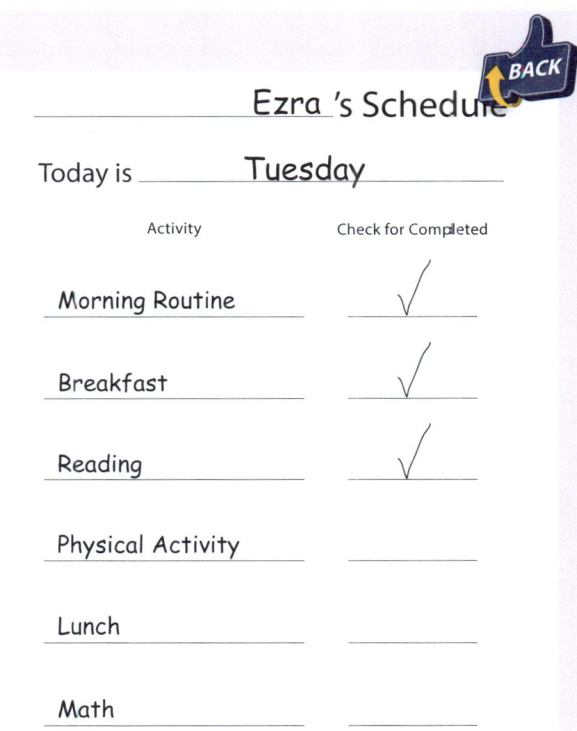

Figure 2.14. This words-only schedule was created in a word processing program, and laminated. Each completed activity is checked off with a dry-erase marker.

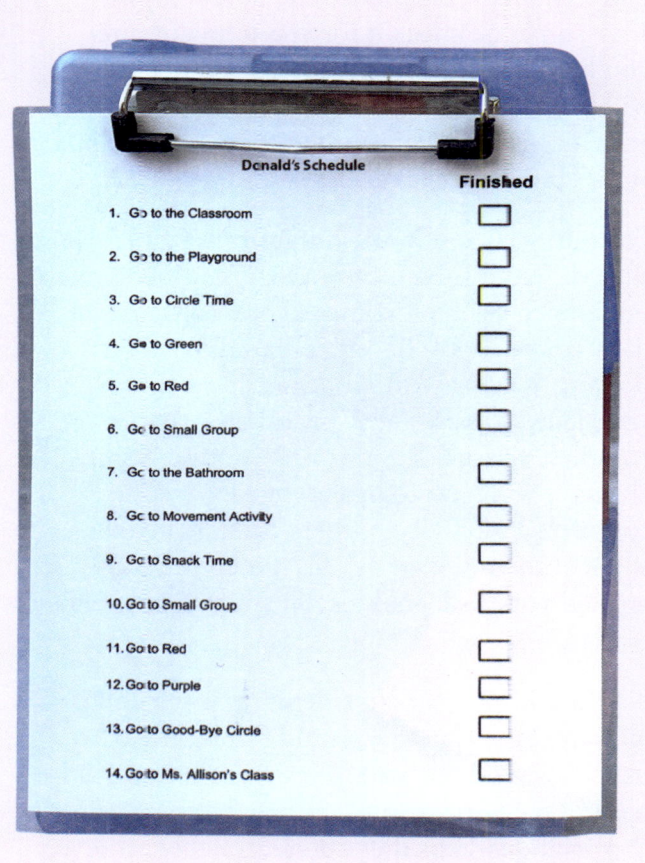

Words schedule selection considerations: An adult would select a words-only schedule for children reading and comprehending the words written for their daily activities. The child should also transition without challenging behavior.

Transitioning to a new schedule style: This style of schedule can follow children into adulthood. It will likely become smaller and more refined like a planner or calendar, but the basic concept will remain unchanged.

Variations: The options for a word schedule are initially fewer than the other styles. However, once a child learns to use this style of schedule, you can transition to many different styles of calendars or daily planners. The images above provide some ideas for this type of schedule.

Visual Schedules

Task Analysis

A task analysis is made by breaking an activity into smaller, more manageable steps, so the child knows each step and the correct order needed to complete an activity. Task analyses will be beneficial until the child can complete each step in the skill independently.

My favorite way, and arguably the best way, to create a task analysis is to complete the activity yourself. As you complete the activity write down each step required to complete the task. Once you have completed the task analysis, have someone check it for you to make sure you have all of the needed steps. I think you will be surprised how many steps everyday activities we take for granted require! Let's look at an example together.

I'm sure your tooth brushing routine looks a little different than mine. We all have personal preferences when it comes to how we complete daily routines. We haven't even talked about flossing, rinsing with mouthwash, washing your face, dressing, and any other activities we complete as part of a morning routine. Some children will have to be taught each step to complete an activity. Others will already have some of the necessary skills. Once you have created your task analysis, let your child try it to determine which steps to teach.

Another important consideration is if a child has any limitation that would inhibit them from completing a step. For example, if a child has physical limitations, create a task analysis that includes steps they can reasonably achieve. If it is impossible to teach a child to cup their hand to put water in their mouth, you teach them to use a cup and make that part of your steps. It is sometimes necessary to be flexible and creative when creating a task analysis for a child. Do not get stuck in what is "normal." Remember, God made us all special and unique with purpose!

Once your task analysis is ready, you can create a visual support of the steps called a mini schedule.

❶ Begin by getting the toothbrush, turning on the water, wetting the toothbrush, and then turning off the water.

❷ Next, retrieve the toothpaste, open the toothpaste container, apply toothpaste to the brush, and close the toothpaste container.

❸ Proceed to brush your teeth; this step can be further broken down into a task analysis of its own.

❹ Following the brushing, turn on the water again, spit out and rinse your mouth, and then turn off the water.

❺ If necessary, repeat the brushing, spitting, and rinsing steps as needed.

❻ Finally, rinse the toothbrush and put it away.*

*Tokens are in the back.

Mini Schedules

Children may sometimes need visual supports broken down into smaller steps than what they see on their visual schedule. These are called mini schedules or schedules within a schedule, and include a task analysis. Mini schedules can be created from a task analysis similar to the example in the previous section. They could also be more general and provide the child with an order of activities. For example, children that have a difficult time with unstructured time frames, such as at a park or on a playground, often benefit from a mini schedule that tells them the order of activities. Perhaps the mini schedule says, "First swing, next slide, then jungle gym." This concept can be used in any setting necessary and be as general or specific as the child needs.

Some children need structure in every setting. Mini schedules can help reduce challenging behavior by providing predictability, but they can also help children that do not initiate play by breaking down the steps even further. You might still need to teach them to do the activities in the different areas, but once they have been taught the necessary skills, the mini schedule will provide the required structure.

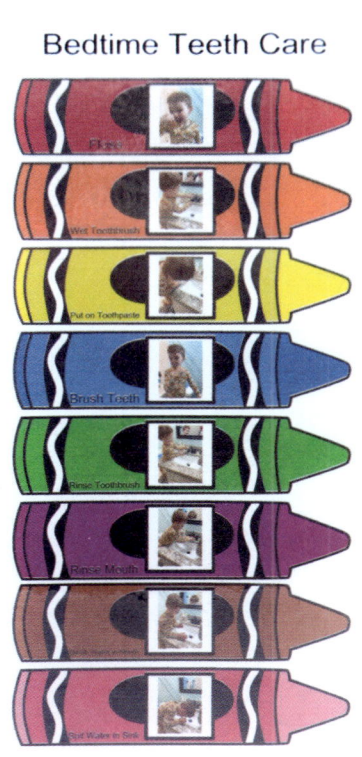

Figure 2.15. This mini schedule visual is created using a word processing program. Photographs of a child modeling the correct actions were inserted next to the words for clarity and a visual model.

Figure 2.16. This task analysis visual is created using a word processing program. The added icons provide visual cues for washing dishes and were created using a program designed to create uniform images for visual supports. It can be laminated for durability

Figure 2.17. This mini schedule shows the order of activities the child will complete during a work session. It was created using a DVD box, icons and Velcro, allowing the activities to be easily exchanged.

Figure 2.18. This task analysis is created using a program designed to create uniform images for visual supports. The visual shows a child exactly what steps to take to use the restroom. This presentation style would suit children who understand reading happens from left to right and top to bottom.

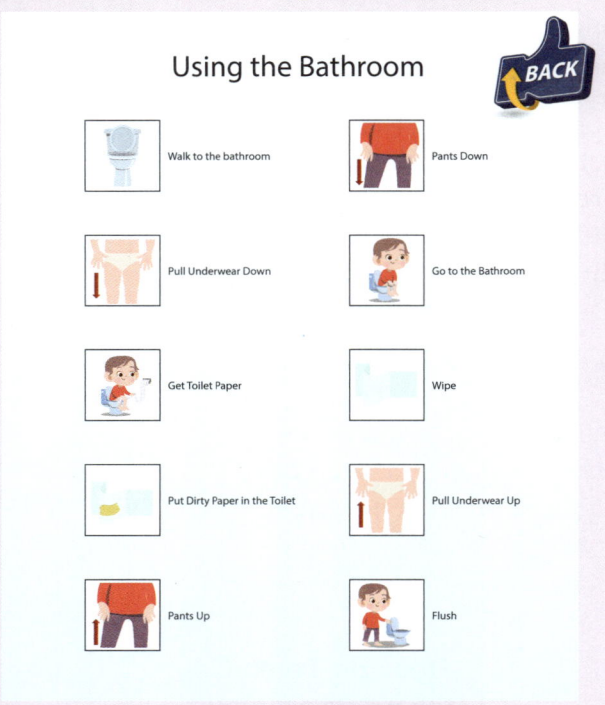

Figure 2.19. This task analysis is created using a program designed to produce uniform images for visual supports. Images are inserted above the words for clarity. This is an example of a chore routine. It reminds the children the steps to cleaning up toys.

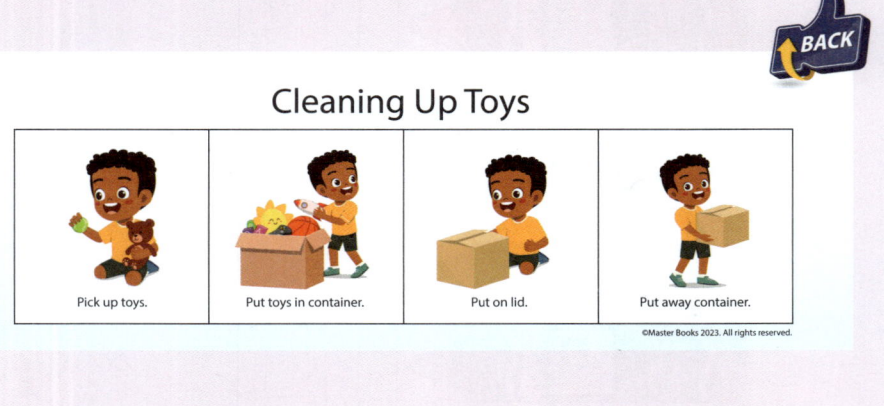

Preparing for Implementation

When you are ready to implement the visual schedule with a child, you will prepare items in advance. First, you will need to determine and gather, if necessary, objects, photographs, icons, or words you will use for a child's schedule. Once you make those decisions, you are ready to begin creating! Following are helpful tips and tricks for visual schedule creation, organization, and storage.

Printing: The majority of the schedule types will require printing. There are a couple of options for consideration. Will you print your photographs with a home printer or use a photo printing service? Will you print your images on cardstock or printer paper?

 **Pro tip:** Cardstock combined with lamination will have a much longer life than paper alone.

Will you laminate checklists and use an erasable writing utensil? Another option is to print out a daily schedule and throw them away after using. A daily printout might be a suitable method if the daily schedule dramatically varies, but beware, it will use a lot of ink!

Figure 2.20. This words-only schedule shows the order of activities the child will complete throughout the day. This schedule shows time to the hour. You can add a checkbox that can be checked with a dry-erase marker if laminated.

7:00 am	Morning Routine
8:00 am	Breakfast
9:00 am	Reading
10:00 am	Chores
11:00 am	Math
12:00 pm	Lunch
1:00 pm	Recess/Free Time

Lamination: Lamination will significantly extend the life of any paper or picture-based visual schedule. A visual schedule can be laminated using a small, portable-sized laminator. If laminating is not available, use transparent packing tape to seal the photographs by taping on both sides of the paper. A third option is to use a page protector. These options allow a child to use a dry or wet-erase marker to check off completed activities. Dry or wet-erase markers enable the writing to be erased, and the schedule to be used the following day.

 **Pro tip:** When you cut out laminated images, leave a small strip of lamination around the cardstock edges. This edge will help keep the edges from peeling and undoing all of your hard work!

Organization and Storage: The images or objects you use for a child's schedule will need to be stored in a convenient location. In my experience, it has been a time-saver to set up an organization system from the beginning of your visual schedule journey. An organization system will help keep images or objects sorted so they can be found when needed. For example, some purchase plastic containers for storage, while others put them in sandwich bags or jewelry holders. Use the storage system that makes sense to you. It does not need to cost a lot of money.

Velcro: Velcro is an essential item for many types of visual schedules. I recommend getting a good pair of scissors that you only use for cutting Velcro and cleaning them after every cutting session. Suggestions for cleaning your scissors include rubbing alcohol, Goo Gone®, and fingernail polish remover, to name a few. You can also purchase special scissors made to cut Velcro! When using Velcro, be sure that you are consistent with how you use the hook (scratchy) and loop (soft) sides. You want to make sure your icons always use one side of the Velcro and the schedule page the other. Otherwise, you wind up with icons that will not stick to your schedule page! I've been there, don't make my mistake!

Extending Visual Schedule Skills

As a child becomes familiar and more independent with their visual schedule, you can add other skills to some visual schedule style variations. Some of these skills can be taught using any schedule style, while others only work with certain schedule types. For clarity, I will note which schedule types can be used to teach each skill following.

Figure 2.21. This image shows a child modeling a surprised face. While you could use a ready-made free image you find on the internet, another option is to have a child make a surprising look to create the photo.

Figure 2.22. The written word "surprise" is another option to use with a child. It could be something you type and print, handwrite, or let a child create and decorate. There are many options!

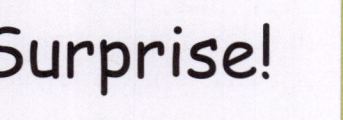

Figure 2.23. The soft puff is an example of an object that could be used to represent surprise. You could use many different objects, just ensure that it does not mean anything else to a child.

Time: If a child is working on telling time, you can add time to their visual schedule to give them additional opportunities to practice. You can make the time component look digital or analog. Just be sure to use the same format you taught. In addition, only add the time increments that a child has mastered to reinforce prior knowledge. For instance, if a child has mastered telling time by the hour, you should use hourly increments on the schedule. You do not want to introduce new time increments on the schedule. You will need to teach them how to use the time component in conjunction with the schedule, but you do not want to teach the skill of telling time. Adding a time component could potentially work with the following visual schedule types: Icons, words with icons, and words-only. My hope is the examples following will give you some ideas on how time can work with a visual schedule.

Accepting change: When using visual schedules with a child, the goal is to stick to the schedule you set for the day. Sticking to the schedule is especially important as they are learning to use visual schedules. However, we all know things happen and sometimes our day does not play out in the order anticipated.

Change is hard for many children with special needs. Children with autism traditionally have a difficult time with transitions and change. One way to teach change is to incorporate "Surprise" into the schedule. Presenting a change in the visual schedule is far easier than having to explain it using words alone. I have heard the same skill taught as "Oh no," and "Change." I am sure some other words or phrases are used, but I find that surprise can cover fun and not-so-fun events. The more critical component is how the skill is taught, although the phrase should be logical and used throughout their lives and is a skill that can be taught with any type of visual schedule. As adults, we know that some surprises are happy while others are sad or unwelcome. Using this strategy, you will be able to teach multiple kinds of surprises. A neutral tone with this strategy helps create space for "Surprise" to mean different things. Teaching a child this skill will allow you to make changes in the future when life happens and you have no other choice than to change the schedule. Accepting change is a life skill that children will use throughout their lives. Accepting change is a skill that can be taught with any type of visual schedule.

When teaching a child to accept change, begin with fun, child preferred activities.[10] You choose an object, icon, image, or word that aligns with the visual schedule style and place it on the schedule on top of the activity space selected. In the beginning, choose an activity they don't mind replacing. Next, you say "Surprise" in a neutral tone while showing the surprise icon or selected photograph. Initially, you want to present a fun, preferred surprise as soon as possible after saying, "Surprise." As a child learns to accept change without any challenging behavior or visible stress, you will change the fun activities for neutral ones. Perhaps they don't love puzzles, but they will do them. That would make a great neutral activity. As before, when a child accepts change with neutral activities, it is time to teach unwelcome or non-preferred change.

When considering what a child might consider unwelcome, you do not want to choose something that will cause great anxiety or grief. We know those events happen sometimes, but we want those to be real surprises that are few and far between. For example, maybe a child loves reading but doesn't enjoy math. Math might be an unwelcome change for them. Perhaps it is raining outside, and you can't go out for exercise today. That could also represent an unwelcome change.

Self-Management: When using self-management strategies, you are teaching a child to manage their behavior. You can target challenging behavior, social skills, life skills, communication, and academics, just to name some potential target areas. Self-management can be used with icons, words with icons, and words-only schedules. Self-management requires the child to have the ability to distinguish appropriate vs. inappropriate behavior. A child will also need to have the skills to follow the schedule with the self-management system, mark their behavior, and provide themselves with reinforcement.[11]

Following are two similar self-management strategies that lend themselves to working in conjunction with visual schedules. Initially, the adult will teach the child how to use the steps of the system and begin to fade out their support as the child becomes more independent using the system. Start small with one target behavior for the child to track. If you want challenging behavior to decrease, provide them with a clear definition of the behavior you do not want to see, then teach and model what you want them to do instead. Then have the child track the use of the replacement behavior you choose. That shifts the focus to the behavior you want to see instead of always bringing attention to the challenging behavior.

Figure 2.24. This datasheet is used to teach children to monitor and recognize their own behavior. There are two target behaviors. At the end of each activity, the child gives themselves a score on the target behaviors using a plus or minus for each. The adult then provides their score to see if they recognized their behavior correctly. Children are given more points for correctly identifying their behavior, which should reinforce correct selection.

	Reading		Chores		Math		Writing		Science		Total Points
	Student	Adult	Student	Adult	Student	Adult	Student	Adult	Student	Adult	
Sitting in Chair	+ −	+ −	+ −	+ −	+ −	+ −	+ −	+ −	+ −	+ −	
Keep Papers Whole	+ −	+ −	+ −	+ −	+ −	+ −	+ −	+ −	+ −	+ −	
Points											

0 points if no match   1 point if the adult scores a +   2 points if both score a +

Next, an adult will score the child at the end of each activity to see if their scores match the scores of the child. If the child and adult give the same score and it is positive (e.g.: yes, plus sign, smiley face), they get 2 points. If the child and adult provide the same score and it is negative (e.g.: no, sad face, minus sign), they get 1 point for telling the truth. Last, if the child and adult score the period differently, the child gets 0 points. The lack of points for falsely identifying their behavior will be important in the future when the adult score matching fades out. The points "buy" previously agreed-upon items or activities that the child finds reinforcing.

After a child has learned to identify if they are following their self-management plan accurately, you will remove the formal adult matching component. You can fade that out by talking with a child after each time they score and provide praise each time they score themselves correctly. Continue to have a points system so they can earn reinforcement. Eventually, you will be able to fade out the adult follow-up component.

I recommend expanding to no more than three target behaviors at a time. However, as a child masters target behaviors and show that they can maintain the skill, you can roll off a mastered skill and introduce a new one.

Figure 2.25. This self-management chart shows an icon schedule. The child selects their score after each activity. The parent will then talk through the score with the child if they need support tracking accurately.

THRIVE: Special Needs Strategies That WORK!

Daily Behavior Tracker

Breakfast	Did I put my dishes in the sink?	Yes	No
Reading	Did I attend during read-aloud?	Yes	No
	Did I attempt to sound out words?	Yes	No
Chores	Did I complete my daily chores?	Yes	No
Math	Did I attend during math?	Yes	No
	Did I work the expected amount of time?	Yes	No
Exercise	Did I complete my exercises?	Yes	No
Science	Did I attend during science?	Yes	No
	Did I complete my work?	Yes	No

Figure 2.26. This words-only chart tracks various target behaviors. The child scores this using a yes/no scale after each activity. Since the target behaviors change with each activity, this would be an example of a child who has advanced beyond needing adult support for accurate tracking.

Teaching visual schedules

Teaching a child to use visual schedules will vary depending on their current skills. Our goal is always that children are as independent as possible. To help a child reach their highest level of independence, you will select prompts based on their needs and the visual schedule style. Reinforcement will also be valuable when teaching a child to use a visual schedule. In Chapter 5, we go in-depth on the value and use of these evidence-based practices. In Chapter 1 we discussed reinforcement, and in Chapter 5 we will go in-depth on the value and use of prompting.

Transition Strategies: Along with prompting and reinforcement, other tools can be helpful when teaching a child to use their visual schedule. Transitions are often difficult for children with special needs. To help reduce a child's reactivity to a transition, we can provide a verbal reminder when it is almost time to transition.[12] Five minutes is a good time to being verbal warnings with a second reminder at one minute. It is also a good idea to use a visual timer along with the verbal warnings. There are different types of visual timers available that provide the visual reminder needed. These are discussed in Chapter 3, Visual Supports. In addition to the verbal reminders and visuals, timers with an end sound are helpful.

When you initially teach visual schedules, it may be beneficial to take the schedule or transition icon to a child instead of transitioning to a central location. As a child becomes proficient with transitioning, you may find a central place to keep the visual schedule. For example, I often see visual schedules hung on walls or doors as a central location. You could continue to use a transition icon if a child needed that support. A final option could be if a child's schedule is on a clipboard, notebook, or another portable item. A portable item would allow them to transport it to any location. When using this option, you should ensure a child can keep track of the schedule.[13]

Teaching steps for visual schedules: The steps to teach a child to use their visual schedule will vary by the transition and schedule type they use. In Chapter 5 you will learn more about prompting, which will be very helpful when teaching a child to use visual schedules. The information from Chapter 1 on reinforcement will also be supportive.

Visual Schedules

1. Give a child a cue to transition. This could be a timer cue (1a) if they can transition independently or a transition icon (1b) if they are not transitioning without adult support. A third option is to bring the schedule to a child (1c). If a child carries their schedule with them, they should already know how to use the steps in a visual schedule or should be able to learn with a general teaching overview.

2. Teach a child to transition to the schedule.

   2.1. (1a) Set a timer to provide an auditory cue when it is time to transition.

       (1b) Hand the child a transition icon when it is time to transition.

       (1c) Bring the schedule to the child.

   2.2. Teach a child how to transition to the location with their schedule.

      2.2.1 Stand behind the child to prompt them. Make sure they are looking at the visual schedule and not you.

      2.2.2 Place the schedule information in the child's hand.

      2.2.3 Use precise language (E.g.: lunch or time for lunch!). Do not use extra, unnecessary language.

      2.2.4 Prompt the child to the area or location coming next. When they arrive, assist them with matching the icon or object (this will depend on the landing zone style chosen, if applicable).

      2.2.5 Have the child stay in the scheduled location until it is time to transition again.

      2.2.6 Repeat steps 2.2.1 through 2.2.5, fading prompts as quickly as possible until the child can transition independently through their visual schedule in the correct sequence.

3. As soon as you know a schedule change will happen, make the change on their schedule and tell them.

THRIVE: Special Needs Strategies That WORK!

Landing Zones and Transition Icons

The landing zone is where a child will place their object or icon when they complete the given task or activity. You can use everyday items to create landing zones. For example, folded pockets made with construction paper, small baskets, and plastic containers with the icon or picture taped to them work well as landing zones.

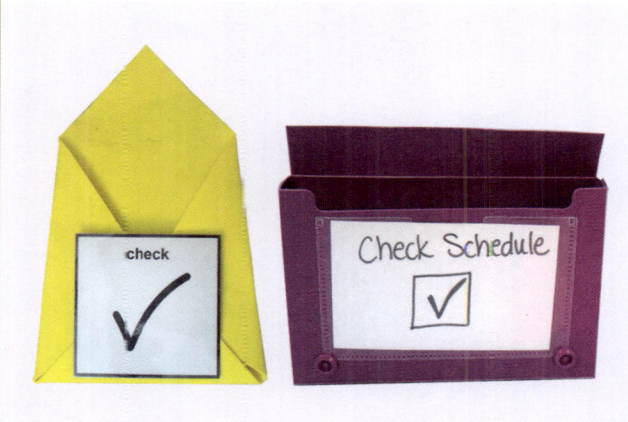

Figure 2.27. This "finished" folder is made with foam paper and a check schedule icon. The plastic container holds icons when a child is finished checking their schedule.

Figure 2.28. This landing zone was created using construction paper, an icon, and Velcro. When the child takes the icon from their schedule, they carry it to the landing zone and place it on the open Velcro.

Figure 2.29. Simple drawing option for a check schedule icon. This example could be an icon or icon with words, depending on how it is created. This icon is created using a program designed to create uniform images for visual supports.

My Schedule

 Wake at 7:00

 Homework

 Music Lessons

 Watch TV

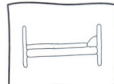 Bedtime at 8:00

Visual Schedules

Figure 2.30. Plain plastic chips are a possible transition token for those using an object schedule.

Figure 2.31. A second option for a check schedule icon created by a program designed to make uniform images for visual supports.

The last tip for teaching transitions is to hand a child an object, icon, or word when the timer sounds. The icon or object should show the message that it is time to check their schedule. The transition icon can help remind your child where they are going as they transition. If they match it to a landing zone, it can solidify they have arrived at the correct location.[14]

These can look many different ways. As long as you are consistent as you teach the routine, the child will learn the icon means it is time to check their schedule. Look above and the prior page to see examples of potential check schedule icons. As with visual schedules, choose the option that works for you and the child.

How do I know if it is working?

Sometimes changes take time to be noticeable to those working with their child day-to-day. There may be minor daily changes that adults do not pick up on because there are so many other challenging behaviors to which they would like to see a difference. When you want to see if a child has learned something you have taught, you take data. When you teach a skill with many steps, such as a task analysis, I recommend a data collection tool that will double as a graph. You can individualize the simple format shown on figure 2:32 for any style of visual schedule. You should note and track a child's type of schedule, the length, the prompts used, and the steps to complete it. I recommend taking data on schedule progress one time per week.

Visual Supports

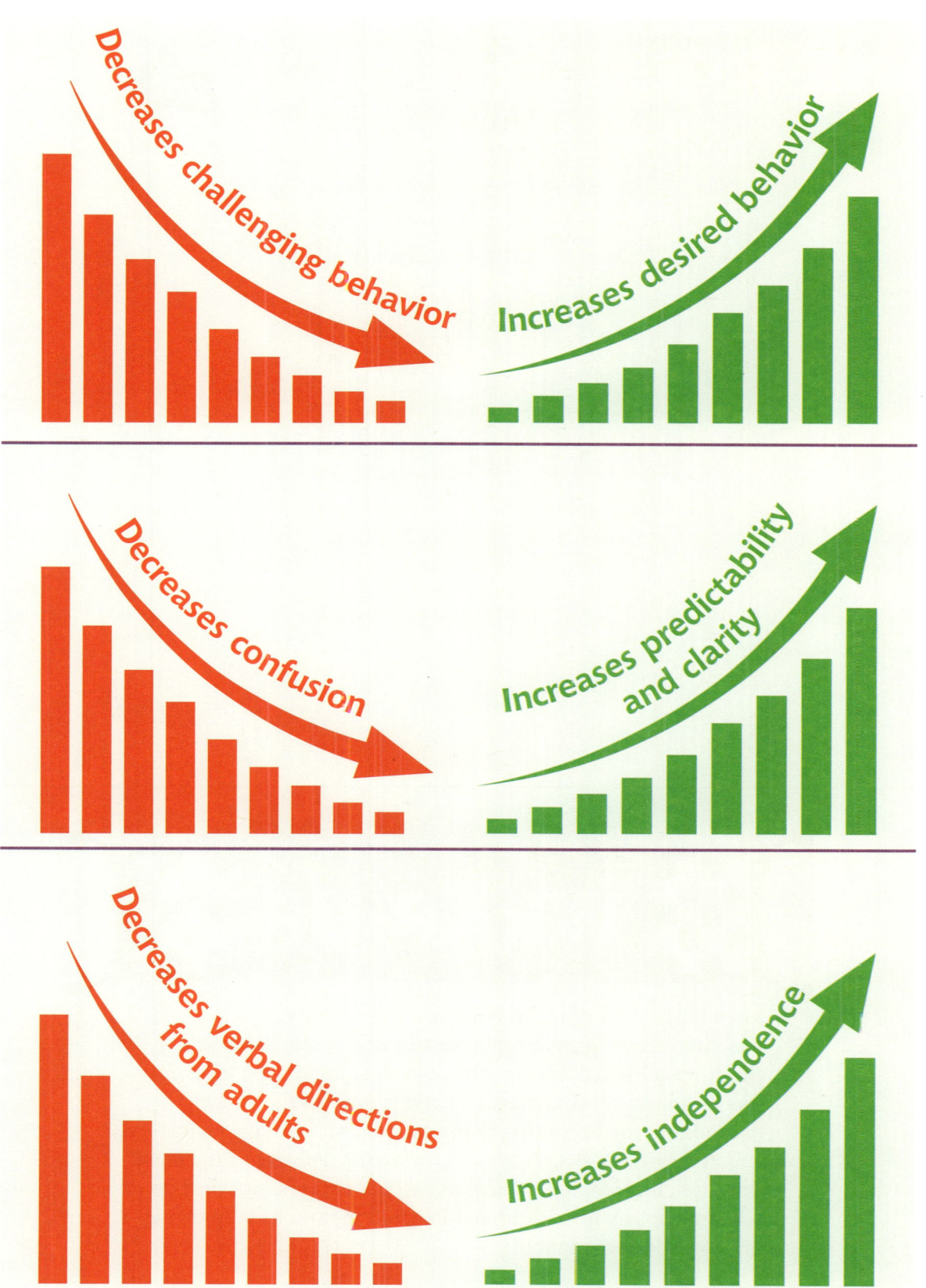

Visual Schedules

Figure 2.32. This data collection sheet can be used for any task analysis. It includes prompting levels and the direction of the teaching steps. It will also double as a graph showing progress when completed.

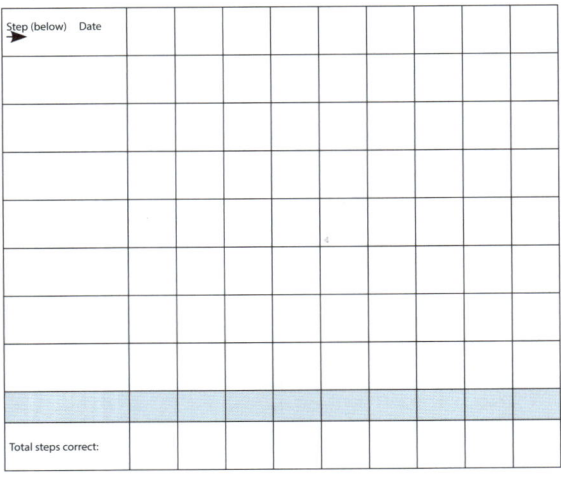

WRAP-UP

My hope for this chapter is that you walk away with a plan for selecting, creating, and implementing visual schedules with a child. Visual schedules are often a foundational need for many special education students. If a child fits any of the guiding questions at the beginning of the chapter, I encourage you to give it a try. The basic structure can grow to incorporate valuable life skills for children. It may take some time to figure out the best schedule option for a child, but I encourage you to keep trying until you find the right fit!

For I know the plans I have for you, declares the Lord, plans for welfare and not for evil, to give you a future and a hope.
—Jeremiah 29:11

Visual Supports

Imagine a world where instructions came without images. I recently put together a bed frame and was surprised when the instructions were only images. There were phrases and labels on the page, but the instructions were not detailed. I quickly matched the parts to the pictures and put the frame together without issues. Now imagine a world with road signs with no arrows and crosswalks without signs showing when it is safe to walk, or being in a foreign country with no pictures or symbols to go along with the text. Some of us would be fine in that world, just slightly inconvenienced. Others would find it much more complex, and some even impossible. You may be wondering if a child needs visual supports. I recommend revisiting the list of questions in Chapter 2 to determine if a child needs a visual schedule.

Visual supports are images paired with verbal instructions that support the comprehension of spoken word(s). Visual supports have many benefits, including clarifying expectations, relaying surprises or routine changes, and providing an additional way to process incoming information. When a person uses visual supports before presenting instructions, the visual becomes an antecedent strategy. Antecedent strategies are essential for reducing challenging behaviors. To use visuals as an antecedent strategy, you put them in place before the behavior occurs. We want visual supports to be readily available and easily accessible. This chapter will look at the types of visual supports I found successful for children in the past.

Teaching Visual Supports

Before we dig into different types of visual supports, I want to give you some general guidelines for teaching them. When presenting directions with visual supports, you should keep your phrases short. Try to reduce filler words that we add as adults. For instance, I would say, "Sit," instead of "I asked you to go sit down!" Additionally, it is essential to say what you want to see instead of what you do not. In schools, I often hear teachers in the hallway yelling, "Stop running!" The last thing the child hears is "running." Instead, tell them what you would like. In this case, "Walk!" would be a more effective phrase. As I previously mentioned, we want to keep a neutral or happy tone and facial expression. Get down on the child's level. Bend or squat within a foot or safe distance of the child so you are on the same level. As a child becomes comfortable with the process, use visuals consistently during the day in different locations and with multiple adults to support generalization.

When teaching a child to use visual supports, follow these basic steps:

1. Show the child the visual.
2. Use specific, concise phrases.
3. Prompt and assist the child with completing the activity while using visual supports so they begin to understand what the visual represents.
4. Positively reinforce the child for completing the task.
5. Fade prompts as quickly as possible.

Sometimes you need to prompt a child through activities or tasks. When a child can independently use the visual, limit your prompts. It is imperative to fade prompts as quickly as possible so a child does not become prompt-dependent.[15] In Chapter 5, we will discuss prompting in greater depth.

Let's dive into some visual supports!

First/Then

The first/then board is a tool used in many ways. It visually represents what a child needs to do first to get to the next item. Many times, that will be an item they find reinforcing. First/then boards can be used before or after challenging behavior occurs. When we use tools and strategies before challenging behaviors occur, we call them antecedent strategies. I prefer to use an antecedent strategy to reduce the possibility of the challenging behavior ever occurring. I am guessing that would be your preference too! Will it always work that way? No, but often it will, especially if you have an item very reinforcing to the child on the "then" side.

A first/then board can be paired with a visual schedule. For example, if a child is using a visual schedule, you might have a first/then board at the table while they work. To use a first/then board, you load the "first" side with a task you would like a child to complete. Second, you place an item they are working toward on the "then" side. Then you say to the child, "First _____. Then _____." That's it! Keep it simple. You can use that phrase multiple times if needed to remind the child what they are working toward, but don't overdo it!

First/then boards can be created using many of the same materials listed in Chapters 1 and 2. You can make them with computer programs, construction paper, or cardstock. I again recommend lamination for durability. You can also add Velcro if you use icons or draw in the boxes with dry or wet-erase markers.

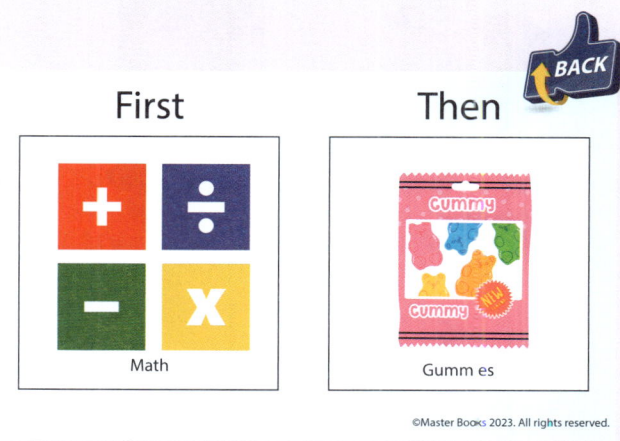

Figure 3.1. First/then boards can be created in many different ways. Once printed (I suggest cardstock), you can laminate the page for durability. This style was printed, laminated, and attached with Velcro.

Figure 3.2. This first/then board was created using construction paper and lamination. The images could be drawn with a dry-erase marker, erased, and changed as needed.

Figure 3.3. First/then boards can be created on storage pouches using a marker, Velcro, and printed images. Extra icons and reinforcers can be kept inside the pouch.

Figure 3.4. A helpful strategy for students who use token boards and first/then boards is to create a token board on one side and a first/then board on the other.

Visual Supports

Figure 3.5. This first/then board has been extended into three steps. There are two work items followed by a reinforcing activity. It was created using cardstock, lamination, and Velcro.

Wait

Waiting is hard. It has become even more difficult as the world has become more digital. Some children will learn to wait through the same methods you and I did. Others will need extra support to learn how to wait. Waiting is an abstract concept that is difficult if you do not understand the concept of time. I will share a systematic way to teach children to wait using visual supports. When you are initially teaching a child to wait, you want to create practice opportunities. However, waiting can also be taught in naturally occurring moments. So if an opportunity comes along, take advantage of it. You do not want to hold up an item and ask them if they want it only to tell them to wait. That would likely not go well! You also must ensure that other toys, items, or activities are unavailable during the practice opportunities.

Determine what visual support you will use when teaching wait. You will also need items a child likes to play with and work toward. When thinking about the value of items, it might help to place them in three categories. Highly preferred items would be favorites, moderately preferred items

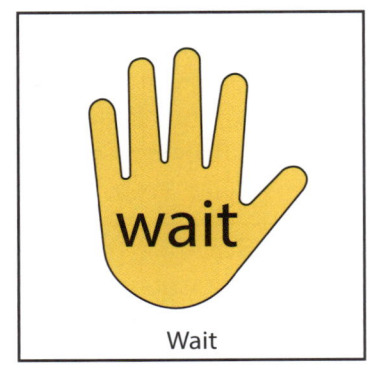

would be items they could take or leave, and non-preferred items are those that they dislike. I recommend beginning with a highly preferred item before asking them to wait for something less enticing. You also need to determine the amount of time you will use with a child to begin. To gain this information, do three "trials." First, ask the child to wait and count the number of seconds they can wait without challenging behavior. Next, take the lowest number and start 3–5 seconds before that to provide a successful beginning. If that means starting with one second, that's okay! You want them to be successful from the start. Finally, you will need a datasheet.

To begin, gather your items:

- Datasheet
- Highly preferred items
- Chosen visual (see figure 3.7 or 3.8)
- Start time identified (the amount of time a child will wait)

Process:

1. You will note the item the student is working toward and whether it is moderately or highly preferred.

2. Note the amount of time a child will wait.

3. Hand the child a wait card, set a visual timer in a location they can easily see, or both.

4. Hopefully, the child will reach your selected amount of time without challenging behavior. If they do, immediately hand them their item and take the wait visuals while they play. While you are handing them the item, say, "Nice waiting!"

5. If challenging behavior occurs during the wait time you chose, stop the timer, wait until the challenging behavior has ended, say, "You are waiting. Try again," and restart the timer. Repeat this process until success is achieved.

6. Set a timer for reinforcement (if it is not an edible treat).

Figure 3.6. This datasheet will allow you to track a child's progress as they learn to wait.

Wait Datasheet

Date	Trial	Item Student Wanted	Wait Time	# of times needed to count	Challenging Behavior Observed

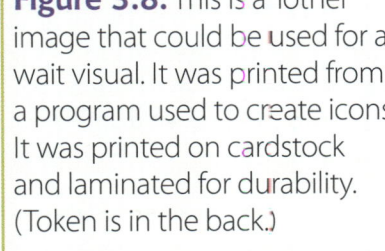

Figure 3.7. This is an image that could be used for a wait visual. It was printed from a program used to create icons. It was printed on cardstock and laminated for durability. (Token is in the back.)

Figure 3.8. This is another image that could be used for a wait visual. It was printed from a program used to create icons. It was printed on cardstock and laminated for durability. (Token is in the back.)

Wait

Wait

Visual Supports

Figure 3.9. Visual timers like the one shown below are great for students that need a visual while waiting. Some make a sound at the end, while others do not.

Break

As an adult with attention deficit hyperactivity disorder (ADHD), I need more frequent breaks while working than most of my coworkers. Children that are unable to communicate their need for a break verbally will often engage in challenging behavior as a way to let you know. One way to prevent that is to teach them to request a break. For this antecedent strategy, you will choose the task the child dislikes the most. You can also use this to discuss body language and help a child identify signals that indicate they need a break. Many children will require you to make that connection for them initially by verbally noting what you see.

You must choose a visual support when preparing to teach a child to request a break. Next, determine how a child will use the card to request their break. Does it make more sense for the child to point to the card or hand you the card? Then select the task or activity you will use to teach the process. Remember to choose something the child does not enjoy. It will make the teaching process easier! Lastly, decide what options will be available during the break. Breaks are not meant to be playtime. They are intended to be a break to regroup and calm down. Sometimes this includes sitting on a beanbag, looking at a book, or doing another calming activity.

Before you begin, show the icon to a child and tell them it is used to request a break. You should also be clear about what a break means. It is a break from work, not playtime. Tell them their options for a break. You will then model how you would like them to use the card to request their break.

1. Place the icon in a place the child can easily reach and use.

2. Begin the activity or task you chose to teach break.

3. Immediately after you present the directions for the activity, prompt the child to request a break. If they need physical support, you can help them pick up the card and place it in your hand using a physical prompt.

4. As soon as the request is made, remove the task and give the child a break. I recommend short breaks (2–3 minutes) and setting a timer to signal the end. Don't forget the verbal reminder when their time is almost up.

Practice this process with a child several times per day. Once they successfully request a break in their least favorite activity consistently without challenging behavior, you can have them practice in others. Like teaching the wait process, you do not stay in this teaching stage long. Once they have it down, begin adding work before granting their break. You may need to start with one item and build from there. For example, they must complete one math problem before getting their break. If a child begins to engage in challenging behavior when you add work, make sure they complete the task(s) before the break. You could also use a first/then board to support you in this situation. As soon as they complete the work, grant their request. Remember to add work back slowly. If you add too much work too quickly, the process could fail. Add a task when they use it independently at the step you are on. If you are prompting their response, they are not independent yet and are not ready for that added task. Every once in a while continue to throw in a break immediately when they request it. Varying the breaks and how fast and frequently they receive them typically strengthens the process.

Break

I Need a Break

Figure 3.10. This is an example of a break visual. It was created using cardstock and lamination. (Token is in the back.)

Figure 3.11. This icon was created using a web-based program for icons. It was printed on cardstock and laminated for durability. It is just one example of what might be used to represent that a break is needed. (Token is in the back.)

Figure 3.12. This break visual support shows the three activities the child and the adult have agreed upon. It also shows the order in which they will complete them. They are attached with Velcro so activities can be changed out as needed.

Figure 3.13. Once a child learns to take a break, they may try to use it to escape work. A great strategy for that behavior is to allow them a set number of breaks during a certain period of time. This visual allows for three breaks during the specified time.

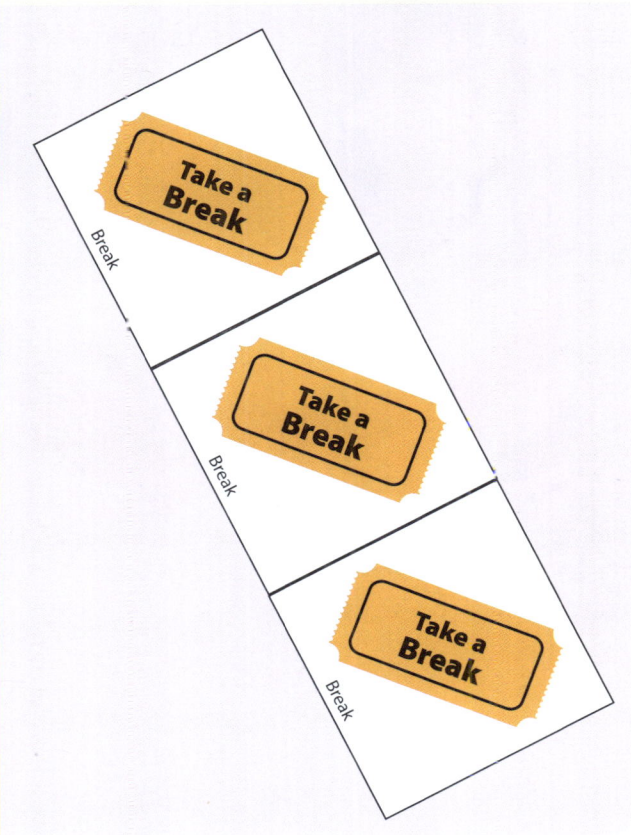

Visual Supports

Help

Just as we have to explicitly teach some children to wait and ask for a break, there are times we need to teach them how to request help. Children will sometimes engage in challenging behavior because they need support, and that is the only way they know to get someone's attention. When preparing to teach a child to request help, you must choose a visual support. First, determine how a child will use the card to request help. Does it make more sense for this child to point to the card or hand you the card? Whichever you choose, be sure to use the same method for teaching other visual supports.

Before you use the icon, show a child and tell them its purpose. Then, store the icon in a place easily accessible to the child. For this process, it is better to use naturally occurring opportunities. When you notice the child getting frustrated, you will teach asking for help.

When you notice an opportunity to teach this skill, you will:

❶ Prompt the child to request help. If they need physical support, you can help them pick up the card and place it in their hand using a physical prompt.

❷ As soon as the request is made, help them with the task.

My one caution with this process is that occasionally a child will ask for help with everything instead of trying to problem-solve or attempt a task. In that case, you can have them try a specified number of times (I would begin with one and stop with three). If a child is ready, you can also have them come up with one or two ways to solve their problem and try before you assist. This could be facilitated through a conversation. You may need to model problem-solving out loud for them initially, then start having them try.

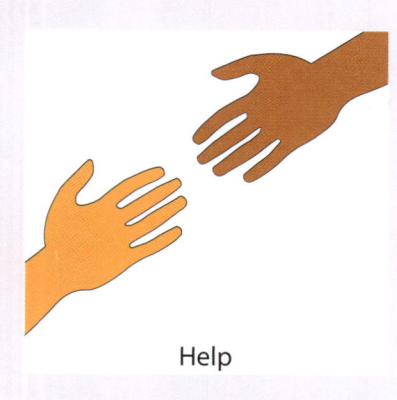

Figure 3.14. This help icon was created using a web program for making icons. It was printed on cardstock and laminated for durability. (Token is in the back.)

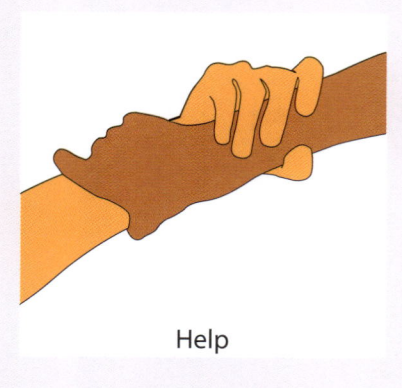

Figure 3.15. Here you see another help icon that was created using a web program for making icons. It was printed on cardstock and laminated for durability. (Token is in the back.)

Timers

Timers are excellent, low-tech support for transitions. When used consistently, timers signal the end of a period so that a child knows a change is coming. For example, timers can end reinforcement time, signal it is time to check their schedule, and show how much time is left during a task or activity. A helpful feature of timers is that, for many children, it takes the "blame" off the parent for stopping a fun activity or reinforcement period. However, sometimes a child does not tolerate the sound a timer makes and becomes agitated. In that case, you can swap to a visual timer that will serve the same function.

Figure 3.16. Timers do not need to be fancy! A simple kitchen timer will do.

Figure 3.17. Another option is to download an app on your device. There are many free options out there. I have had success with the Visual Countdown Timer. It is free and available for Apple or Android.

Portable Visuals

A portable visual is a set of visual support cards that have been laminated and put on a binder ring. These visuals are kept with the adult so you always have access to visual support no matter where you are. Some adults wear them on lanyards, while others put them in their pockets. The key is to have them with you when you need them. I recommend creating a list of the top ten demands you use with your child and making the visuals based on your list. You do not have to have ten, but I would not recommend using many more than that, as your stack will get thick and not be quick to use.

Standard portable visual cards:

- Feet on floor
- Stand up
- Sit down
- Walk
- Shhhh
- Finished
- Clean up
- Bathroom
- Yes
- No

Always make a list that works for you. To create these portable visuals, you can use a program designed for creating icons, have a child model and take a picture, or use clip art. I recommend printing on cardstock and laminating them for durability. Finally, you will punch a hole and put them on a binder ring. A final option is to purchase a set that has already been created.

Figure 3.18. This portable visual set was created using a program designated for creating icons. It was laminated and put on a binder ring. The binder rings can then be attached to wearable connectors for easy travel.

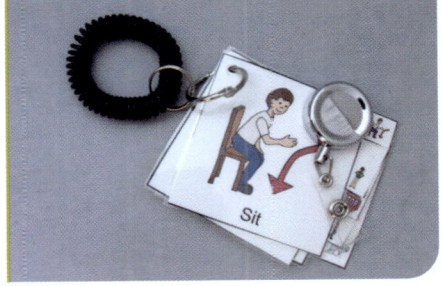

Visual Supports

Visual Boundaries

Sometimes children have a difficult time recognizing boundaries and staying within them. A quick and straightforward strategy for these children is to create a visual boundary. If you have an area a child gets in that you would like to block, you can use fabric to cover the area and make a visual barrier. My favorite way to create visual boundaries is to take colorful tape and outline boundaries for the child. The key is to make your boundary expectations crystal clear and follow them consistently. To do this, take a child to the area and introduce the essential aspects of the boundary. Tell them what activities are appropriate for that area and give them examples of things you would do there. You can also show examples of behaviors you do not want to see in those areas. Sometimes kids really like making videos like this.

Figure 3.19. If you have more than one child you are teaching or need the space for another reason, you could create a visual boundary by taping the section off the table.

Figure 3.20. Another idea is to use tape to make boundaries for a chair on the floor.

Figure 3.21. Any type of fabric can be draped over unavailable items.

Figure 3.22. This barrier was created using a curtain and curtain rod.

Video modeling can also be an effective tool. Have the child model expectations, video it, and use it when needed. When you see the desired behaviors in that area, provide the child with positive reinforcement using the strategies discussed in Chapter 1.[16]

Figure 3.23. A folding screen could be a fantastic barrier for your educational space.

THRIVE: Special Needs Strategies That WORK!

Labels

As we discussed in Chapter 2, labeling is a way to support pre-literacy and build vocabulary for children already reading. With visual supports, labeling is essential for more than just schedules. Labeling can be words only or words with pictures. Labeling can increase independence by showing a child where items are stored to retrieve or help clean up. They can also support children in gaining meaning from items and locations by partnering an image with a word and an action when you show them how the item is used.

Figure 3.24. These were created to label items in the environment. (Tokens are in the back.)

table	window
chair	door
computer	off
on	sink
bathtub	TV
wall	picture
couch	bed

Figure 3.25. These labels can be used on storage containers to organize the learning area. (Tokens are in the back.)

	Building Toys		Dominoes
	Blocks		Wind Toy
	Gear Toys		Puzzle
	Bears		Yo-yo

Social Emotional Skills

Visual supports are very effective in supporting the teaching of social emotional skills. There are many different ways to teach social skills but very few evidence-based curricula out there. However, if you use evidence-based strategies such as the ones in this book, you are covered!

There are many skills that adults might not consider curriculum or skills that must be taught. Social emotional skills are not intuitive for many people and can sometimes fall by the wayside for children if they do not learn them from interacting with others. However, these skills are very important and often must be taught explicitly. In this section, I will share some visual supports for aiding students as they learn to interact with others and even helping them identify feelings and replacement behaviors for themselves. The examples are not exhaustive, but my hope is that you will get ideas that you can incorporate into the child's routines and activities.

Identifying Emotions

Identifying emotions can be very difficult for some individuals with disabilities. One way to begin teaching the concept of emotions is to use images. I prefer icons when I begin teaching this skill because people often have different expressions in real life, which makes it more complex. However, if you come across a real-life situation of an emotion you have practiced, point it out and talk about it. Once they learn the concept by using icons, you want to transition to photographs and real people.

Figure 3.26. This page of icons was created using a web-based icon program. It was printed on cardstock and laminated for durability. Depending on a child's learning needs, you may start with one image at a time or a page similar to this one.

Identifying Emotions and Coping Strategies

Once your child has learned to identify an emotion, if they struggle with emotional regulation, a great strategy is to plan and practice alternatives to how they are currently handling it. On the following page I show an example of what a child can do if they are sad. These options should be selected by the child and practiced when the child is not upset. The visual can be used to present the child with options while they are upset instead of speaking. If a child is already upset, adding a lot of words will potentially overwhelm them further.

Social Narratives

Another excellent strategy for supporting children through emotions is the use of social narratives, also known as social stories. Social narratives are an evidence-based practice for individuals with autism and have been shown to support communication, social behavior, play, and more.[17] As a classroom teacher, I used social stories often with all of my students with disabilities and found them to be effective for most of them no matter the disability. There are many social stories available for free online with a simple search. However, it is quick and easy to create a story on your own.

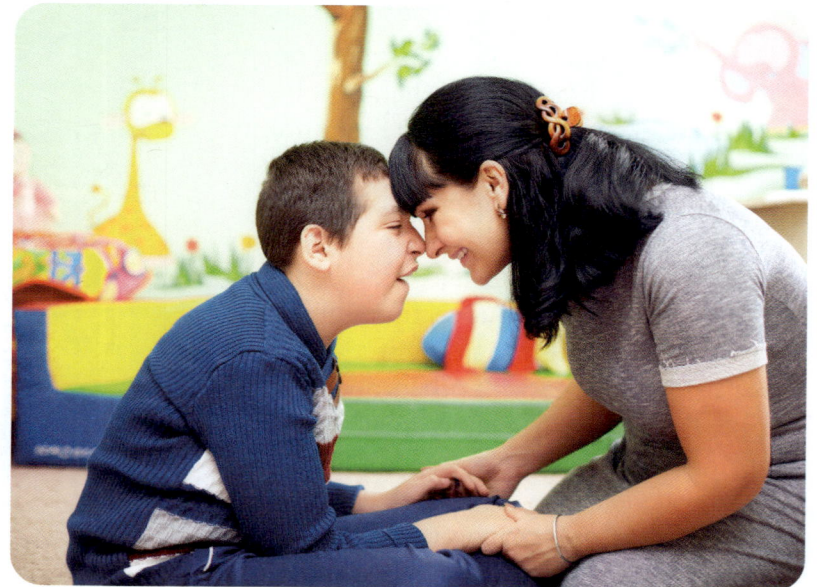

Creating a social story typically begins with the onset of a problem that is not going away. To create a social story, we take that problem and provide alternative behaviors we would like to see. Following are two examples of social stories.

THRIVE: Special Needs Strategies That WORK!

Figure 3.27. This image was created in a program for creating icons. It is a valuable tool for reminding children of their options when they are in the middle of a difficult emotion.

Figure 3.28. This social story was about a child not getting the flavor of cupcake hoped for and what he or she could do instead. It is held together by paper clips and can be created for specific concerns a child faces.

Figure 3.29. The social story in this image was created to give a child options on what they can do instead of biting others. (Token is in the back.)

Visual Supports

Conversation Visuals

If a child has difficulty having conversations with others, visual supports can be beneficial. There are different ways that visuals can support conversations in different locations. We will look at a few examples below.

Figure 3.30. This visual is a board of a few basic words a child might use in a park or on a playground if they are not communicating vocally.

Figure 3.31. This visual support is a one-sheet reminder for staying on topic during a conversation. This would be especially supportive for a child that only likes to talk about one or two things and dominates conversations.

Figure 3.32. These menu cards could be taken to restaurants so that a child can tell you what they want if there are not images on the menu. Additionally, they could use the visual to order their own food!

THRIVE: Special Needs Strategies That WORK!

Data

How do I know if any of the strategies are working?

Data collection truly is the only way to verify how well an intervention works. When we estimate, the actual numbers rarely turn out to be what we thought they would be. Using the datasheet below, you can collect data on the effectiveness of any of the visual supports. To do this, select the behavior you are targeting. For example, are you working to reduce the number of times a child gets out of their seat? You will define the behavior at the top and note the intervention you teach. You will then select an amount of time you will use to collect your data and the activity you are completing.

Pro tip: Collect data using the same process for three days before beginning the intervention so you can see if there is an immediate change.

You will then collect your data and calculate a percentage. After the intervention, your goal is to see that percentage get smaller. Sometimes we do not notice small changes when we are in the moment. This style of data collection will allow you to see those small changes. Make sure you track your data as it happens. Do not fill it in later with guesses, or it will likely be inaccurate.

Figure 3.33. This is a partial interval datasheet. It will allow you to see small changes in a child's behavior.

Visual Supports

Teaching and nurturing children in a biblical way is a sacred and rewarding journey. The Bible offers invaluable guidance and encouragement for parents in this vital role. Consider reading these verses each day to keep your heart full of God's purposes and plans for your life:

Proverbs 22:6 advises, "Train up a child in the way he should go; even when he is old he will not depart from it."

This verse reminds parents that their efforts in imparting godly wisdom and values to their children will have a lasting impact. Even though the results may not be immediately visible, your commitment to teaching them the right path will bear fruit in due time.

Deuteronomy 6:6-7 underscores the importance of constant spiritual teaching: "And these words that I command you today shall be on your heart. You shall teach them diligently to your children, and shall talk of them when you sit in your house, and when you walk by the way, and when you lie down, and when you rise." This passage emphasizes the significance of integrating faith into everyday life, making God's word a natural part of your family's conversations and activities.

Moreover, take comfort in knowing that God is your ultimate source of strength and guidance as you navigate the challenges of parenthood. Isaiah 41:10 assures, "fear not, for I am with you; be not dismayed, for I am your God; I will strengthen you, I will help you, I will uphold you with my righteous right hand." Lean on God's promise to support you in your role as a parent, and trust that He is with you every step of the way.

In moments of doubt or weariness, remember that your efforts in teaching your children spiritually and biblically are a profound act of love and devotion. Your influence as a parent has the potential to shape their lives in ways that extend far beyond the present, echoing into eternity. Keep praying, keep teaching, and keep nurturing their faith, knowing that you are fulfilling a sacred calling that brings blessings not only to your children but to your family as a whole.

WRAP-UP

Adults use visual supports daily, and we consider ourselves to be independent. Our visuals may differ from what our children need, but their impact remains evident. I hope this chapter has provided a starting point for you to brainstorm other visual supports that might assist a child in becoming more independent!

I will instruct you and teach you in the way you should go;
I will counsel you with my eye upon you.

—Psalm 32:8

4

Basic Learning Skills

Imagine you are going to a new restaurant. You are excited to walk in and be seated. You are anticipating the server collecting your beverage and food order. You walk up to the restaurant and open the door. As soon as you step around the corner, a woman behind the counter yells at you in a loud voice, "WHAT'S YOUR ORDER?" You stand there, frozen, trying to look at the menu on the wall above the woman. "WHAT'S YOUR ORDER?" she yells again. Anxiety fills you as you try to scan the menu faster, but you can't focus. Your heart is pounding, you are breathing fast, and you have a ringing sound in your ears. You step back into the foyer, take a deep breath, and slow your breathing. You are utterly unprepared because you have never been to a restaurant like this. You watch what others are doing as they move through the line and browse the menu from afar. When you are prepared, you step into the line to place your order. As soon as you step in, the woman in the back yells, "WHAT'S YOUR ORDER?" You are so far back in line that you must scream your order back to her. As the line moves forward, you pay and go to an empty table to wait for your food. Whew!

Maybe that story does not give you anxiety, but I feel it! As an adult with ADHD, it was completely overwhelming when I had this experience in college. As a 23-year-old, I had years of previous restaurant experience. One change in expectations and I froze. Thankfully, as an adult, I knew I should step back, watch what was happening, and make a plan before moving back in the line to order. Had I ever visited again, I would have known what to do the next time I walked in. Now imagine you are a child with a disability who does not have the skills to step back and make a plan when facing a new scenario. What happens? Each individual will react differently, but you might see challenging behaviors like yelling or running, or maybe they shut down and fall to the floor.

Was visiting that restaurant a negative life-changing experience? No, but I still remember how I felt almost 20 years later! Now, you may be asking, "Jenny, this is a book about teaching children with special needs; why are you telling me about a restaurant?" Because this chapter is about teaching children foundational skills that will allow them to navigate many life circumstances and set the foundation for independence. To do that, we need to consider all the skills we take for granted that we might not remember learning as a child. I call these "learning to learn skills." Executive function and creating routines are additional ways we will look at supporting foundational learning skills needed for life.

Learning to Learn

Learning to learn behaviors are skills many children develop as they encounter the world around them. These foundational skills are critical behaviors children need to succeed in a learning environment, no matter the setting. Learning to learn behaviors are also vital foundational skills to be built upon as children learn and grow. Additionally, they are necessary for preparing a child for independence. While it is not always the case, children with special needs often need to be directly taught one or more of these skills.

There are two categories I follow when teaching essential learning to learn skills. As I share these categories, I will review how the skill supports children, give examples, suggest how to teach them, and call back to the importance of reinforcement from Chapter 1.

1. Motor/Object Imitation

Motor imitation is copying a motor movement after watching another person complete it. For example, I wave, and my 2-year-old watches me and begins to wave. Motor imitation requires a child to pay attention to another individual and copy the same physical action they observed. Imitation can be with or without objects. When imitation is completed using objects, it is called object imitation. Object imitation is more complicated than motor because a child must pick an item up and then complete the imitation. Imitation is a necessary skill for learning to play, engaging socially, and communicating with others. As adults and peers speak, children watch. They notice facial expressions and gestures paired with the words they hear. They watch how others socially engage with one another and how they play with toys. Those observations can turn into new skills when children can imitate motor movements.

Examples of motor/object imitation:

❶ *Beginner level* – With beginner level imitation, you use the same direction ("Do this" in these examples) and a simple one-step direction.

- Adult: Says, "Do this," while clapping their hands together.
- Child: Claps hands together.
- Adult: Says, "Do this," while touching nose with one finger.
- Child: Touches nose with one finger.

- ❷ *Mid-level* – You can advance to simple two-step directions by making imitation a small step harder.

    - ➔ Adult: Says, "Do this," while standing up and then sitting down.
    - ➔ Child: Stands up and then sits down.
    - ➔ Adult: Says, "Do this," while first putting a block in a cup, then picking the cup up and shaking it.
    - ➔ Child: Puts a block in a cup, then picks up the cup and shakes it.

- ❸ *Advanced level*

    - ➔ Adult: Says, "Copy me," while first putting both arms up straight in the air and then touching both knees.
    - ➔ Child: Puts both arms straight up in the air and then touches both knees.
    - ➔ Adult: Says, "Do the same," while alternating hand slaps on the table three times.
    - ➔ Child: Alternates hand slaps on the table three times.

2. One-step Directions

Our days are full of others asking us to comply with directions. "Can you pass the salt?" "Will you hand me the remote?" "Pick that up off the floor!" If you pause and consider the number of one-step directions we encounter daily, I believe you will be surprised because it has become second nature. Therefore, following one-step directions is another vital skill children need to succeed in every environment. You might notice that one-step directions are a component of the directions given for motor imitation. However, they include a modeling prompt for the child. In this section, I am solely addressing verbal directions.

Examples

- ❶ *Beginner level* – When teaching beginner level one-step directions, you should begin with a task that is easy for the child to complete.

    - ➔ Adult: Says, "Clap hands."
    - ➔ Child: Claps hands together.

    - ➔ Adult: Says, "Touch nose."
    - ➔ Child: Touches nose with one finger.

- ❷ *Mid-level* – You can advance to more difficult one-step directions by making the direction a small step harder.

    - ➔ Adult: Says, "Color the circle (on a sheet)."
    - ➔ Child: Colors the circle.

    - ➔ Adult: Says, "Walk with me."
    - ➔ Child: Walks with the adult.

- ❸ *Advanced level* – In the advanced level, you can begin to request that the child follow simple two-step commands.

    - ➔ Adult: Says, "Go grab a paper towel and bring it back to me."
    - ➔ Child: The child gets a paper towel and takes it to the adult.

    - ➔ Adult: Says, "Give grandma a hug and a kiss."
    - ➔ Child: The child gives grandma a hug and a kiss.

Basic Learning Skills

Routines

As we continue down the path of developing independence, routines are next on the list. Jun Kohyama discovered that good daily habits formed during the early stages of life could determine success. A routine is a daily habit that happens frequently and in the same or similar sequence of activities with a beginning and end point.[18] Many valuable life skills are learned through daily routines, including, but not limited to, self-control, organization, self-help skills, social skills, and independence. In addition, the structure and predictability of routines reduce the occurrence of power struggles and can ease transitions.

Routines can happen in any setting. Settings in which I have often seen routines that are helpful to children and families include church, home, school, restaurants, and even the park or other community locations. You can incorporate a routine anywhere a person is frequently expected to do the same activity or steps.

To get your creative thoughts flowing, below is a list of potential routines that could be incorporated into a daily schedule. This list is by no means exhaustive, but it may help you think of other areas that would be helpful.

Examples of routines:

- Transitioning between locations
- Completing independent work
- Picking up toys
- Loading a dishwasher
- Going to the bathroom
- Handwashing
- Eating a snack
- Going to a movie
- Playing a game with peers
- Going to the grocery store
- Crossing the street
- Getting off the bus
- Bedtime
- Getting dressed
- Eating a meal
- Getting in the car

One-step Directions Teaching Tips

As mentioned before in the beginner level examples, when you ask children to complete one-step directions, start with something they will be successful with and can do easily. As with teaching imitation, you will want to pair success with reinforcement. Keep your requests short. As adults, we tend to add many unnecessary words when speaking. Finally, pause and give the child a chance to respond. When your child does not respond, the prompting section in Chapter 5 will be supportive.

Topics from other chapters that support teaching this skill:

Chapter 1: A Positive Environment

Chapter 3: Visual Supports

Tips for Teaching Routines

In Chapter 2, I wrote how a task analysis could assist teaching and learning by breaking a task down into steps and provided an example of a task analysis for brushing teeth. It will be essential to complete a task analysis for each routine so that the same steps are taught, regardless of which adult is assisting the child. I recommend heading back to Chapter 2 for a quick review of task analyses if it is not fresh on your mind before getting started with routines.

When teaching a child to complete routines, it is essential to remember not to rush. Some routines will take a long time for your child to master, which is okay! Select one routine to begin. If you desire to work on two at a time, I recommend they be at separate times of the day. For example, a getting dressed routine in the morning and a bedtime routine. Separating the routines with time will help keep a child from getting steps from the two routines mixed up. After you have completed the steps from Chapter 2 for setting up a routine using a task analysis, you may need to create visual supports to aid in teaching a child the routine. Chapter 5 will explore prompting and different levels of support, including visuals to help make that decision.

Before you begin, prepare your datasheet so you can track growth. The datasheet designed for a task analysis in Chapter 2 is perfect for routine tracking. You only need to collect routine data one time per week. Do it the same day each week to make it easier to remember. The day you collect data, do not provide any prompts. You want to track what a child can do alone. If a child is not motivated to complete the routine, a token board, as described in Chapter 1, can be used to provide the needed outside motivation. If you find that a child can complete the routine with a motivator in place, you will not need to teach the routine. Keep the motivation in place until they are ready for you to fade it out as discussed in Chapter 1. If they cannot complete the routine, you will locate the last step they can independently complete and begin there. Then you will need to teach a child how to complete that next step using prompts (see Chapter 5).

Examples of Visual Supports for Routines

Figure 4.1. This chore routine was created by taking photographs of the child completing the task appropriately. The photos were uploaded into a program for creating icons. The image is posted in a location near where the chore happens. One that is similar can be found in the back of the book.

Figure 4.2. A check-off morning routine can support those who get off task attempting to complete an activity with multiple steps. This checklist was created with a word processing program. Lamination is recommended for durability.

Basic Learning Skills

Figure 4.3. Some children will need to break tasks down into even smaller steps. For example, "getting dressed," as shown in the visual support here, may not be enough information for some. For those kids, break that task down into a set of steps to support success with independence.

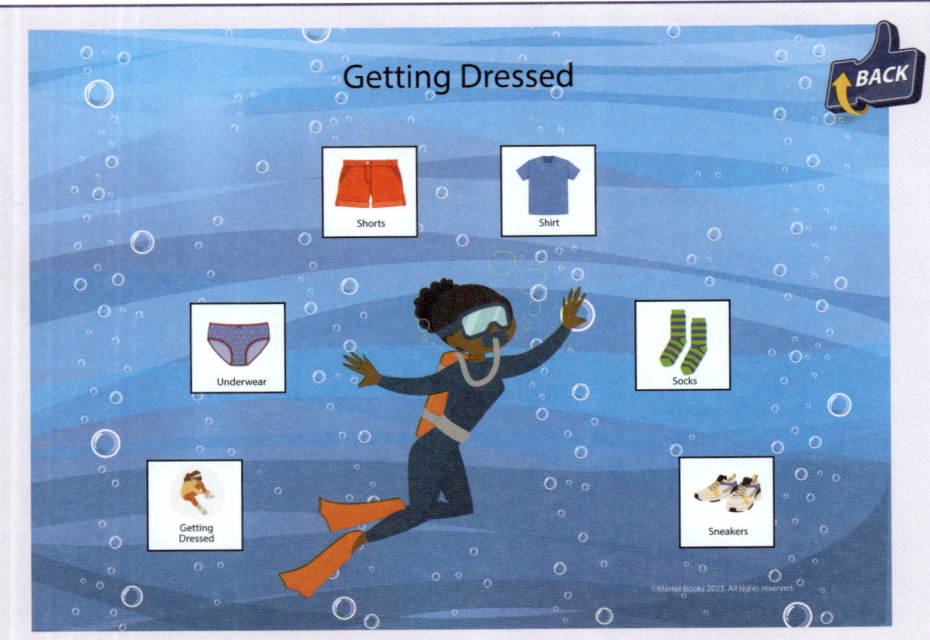

Figure 4.4. Anything can be made into a visual support! Recipes become more accessible when created in a series of images for those that struggle with reading.

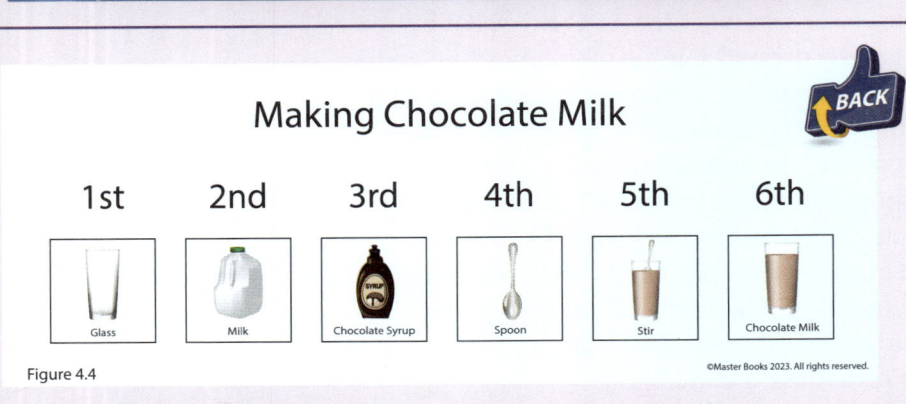

Figure 4.5. This is an example of a voice scale with potential emotion icons at both ends of the scale.

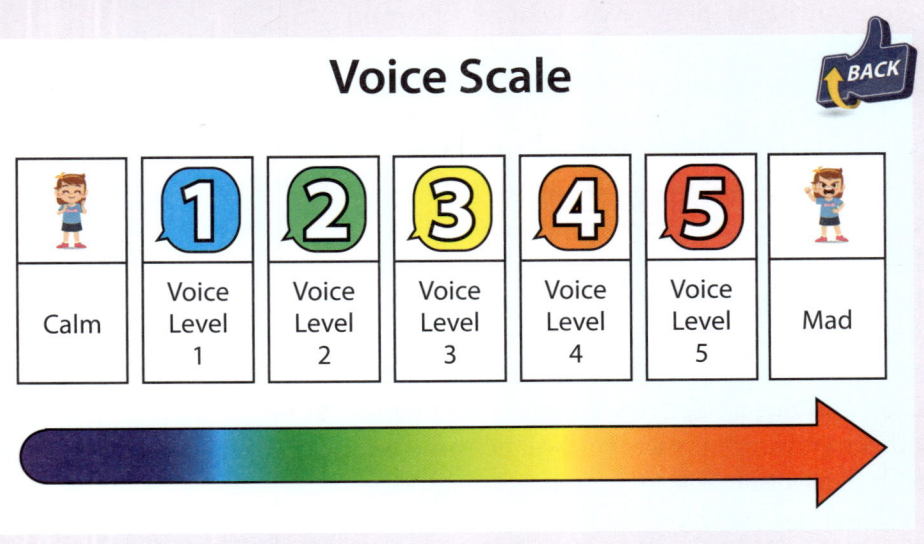

Figure 4.6. Cleaning routines are another idea for a routine-based visual support. This can be created for any room and number of tasks.

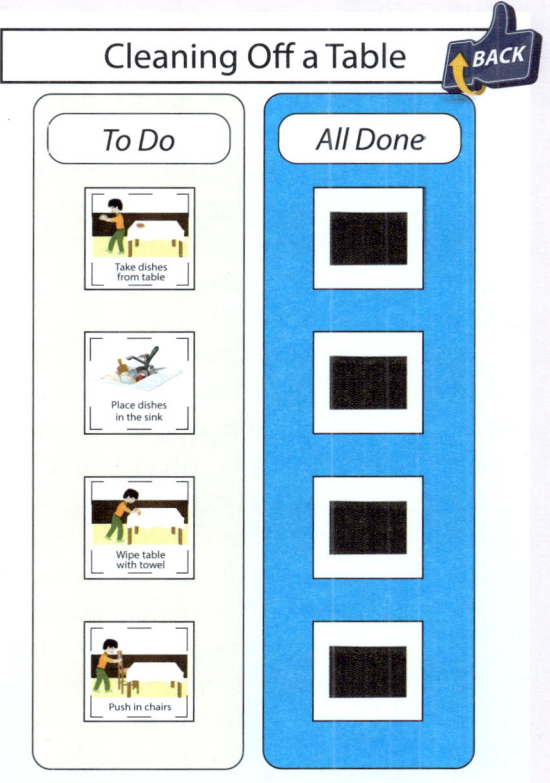

Figure 4.7. Create cards that show a child what to do when they are upset instead of focusing on what not to do. (Token is in the back.)

Additional Life Skills

As you begin to break down tasks for teaching and recognize the number of skills required to complete what seems like a simple daily task, you will see everything through a new lens. It is crucial to consider the mental processes a person must use to complete a task. These skills go by many names: executive function, cognitive processes, executive skills, and executive control are the most common. The vital information to take away here is that these are essential life skills for navigating school, relationships, self-care, and eventually managing a household and working. I will call them essential life skills in this text because they support everything we do in life, including academics.[19]

Essential life skills are developed throughout life; they are not guaranteed. When considering these essential life skills for children with special needs, we will need to be diligent in planning and directly teaching these skills and providing ample practice opportunities. In this section, I will highlight several essential life skills that I have found especially important for children with special needs. Individuals typically have varied strengths and needs when considering these skills, so you may find skills your child excels at and others you plan on supporting immediately.

Organization

Learning to organize is a valuable life skill. We organize many things throughout the day. Our schedule, thoughts, new information, old information . . . the list goes on and on. Teaching children how to organize will support them as they learn to clean their bedrooms, complete household chores, organize their thoughts to tell a story, keep up with items, plan their day, and so much more.

Ways to teach and help a child practice organization:

- Use a visual schedule (Chapter 2).
- Practice sorting items that belong together (e.g.: silverware or laundry).
- Practice retelling a story during reading instruction.
- Create checklists (Chapter 3).
- Break tasks into steps — task analysis (Chapter 3).
- Implement daily routines.

Time Management

Many adults struggle with time management, but we need this skill for so many daily tasks. Learning how to manage time will assist children in their current life and the future. For instance, it helps us know how many activities we can do in one day, how long it takes to get to a location, how long to allow for cooking dinner, and how much time we need to read a chapter of our favorite book. Time management goes hand in hand with organization when considering planning a daily schedule and setting goals.

Ways to teach and help your child practice time management skills:

- Teach a child to tell time when appropriate.
- Have a child guess how much time it will take to complete an activity and review it at the end.
- Use timers (Chapter 1).
- Tell a child what time you have to be somewhere, talk about how long it takes to get there, and do the math to know what time you need to leave.
- Give a child verbal time reminders as they complete an activity (e.g., "We have five minutes left") (Chapter 1).
- Implement daily routines (do you see a trend here?).

Planning/ Prioritizing

Learning to plan and prioritize are more examples of essential skills that we use daily. Planning involves recalling the necessary components to complete a task. Thinking about time is important for identifying when the task needs to happen or how long it will take to complete. Planning often involves making a list showing the order that components should be completed to finish a task. Additionally, once the components or tasks have been determined, they must be prioritized. For example, it would be important to put your socks on before you put on your shoes. Recipes are a great example of planning and prioritizing. If you take the time to think through all the tasks you complete in a day, you will be surprised at how often we use these skills.

Ways to teach and help your child plan and prioritize:

- Practice with them using familiar tasks.
- Draw representations if a child is not reading yet (Chapter 3).
- Teach sequencing with pictures and then transition to words.
- Teach prioritizing using examples that have an obvious response (see the shoe example).

THRIVE: Special Needs Strategies That WORK!

Emotional Control

Controlling our emotions is something we learn to master as we learn and grow. As with the other essential life skills in this section, individual skills and development will vary by individual. Emotional control is vital to remaining calm when encountering obstacles. A lack of emotional control can present as over-excitement, shutting down, and many other ways, based on the individual.

Ways to teach and help a child with emotional control:

- Visuals
- Scales
- Practice emotional learning
- Calming strategies

Figure 4.8. A second example of a voice scale that uses colors to indicate levels, but adds descriptor words.

Figure 4.9. Looking in a mirror to practice identifying and making expressions that go along with feelings is a strategy that supports some children.

Basic Learning Skills

Figure 4.10. Many calming strategies can be found on the internet: Let a child try them and select the ones they find helpful. Create images to remind them what to do when they are upset.

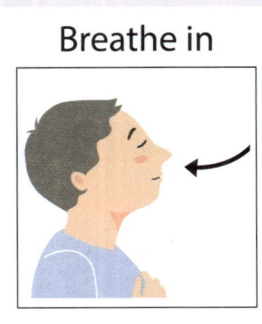
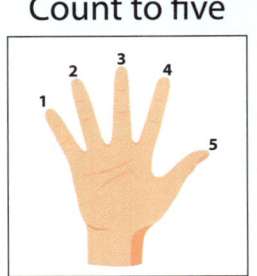
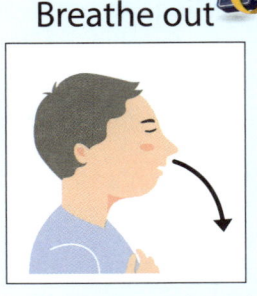

Figure 4.11. Note-taking organizers come in many forms. For children that struggle with fine motor, typing is an option. Another way some students prefer taking notes is by drawing pictures.

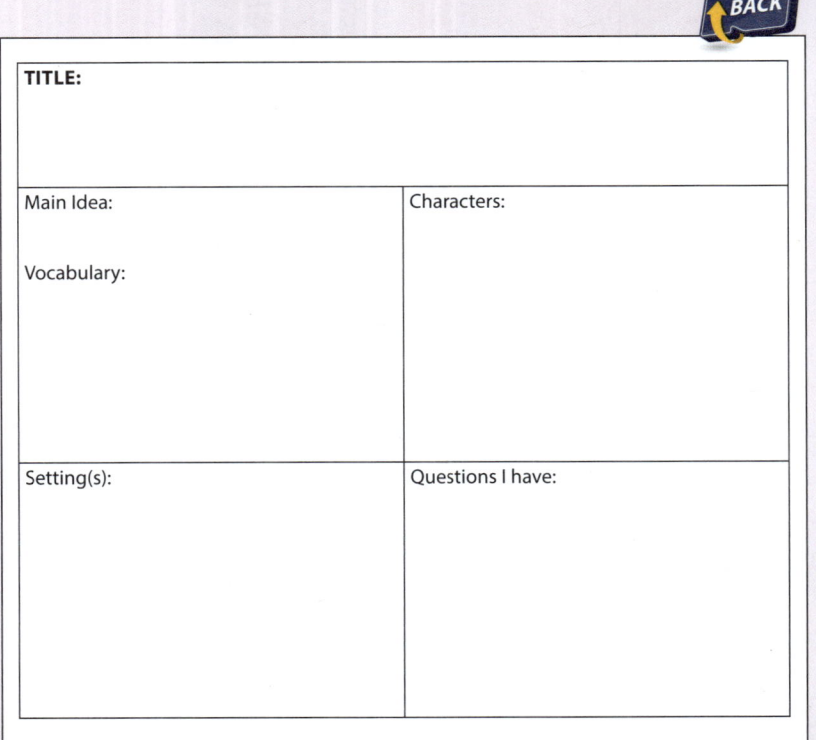

Working Memory

At different times in our lives, many of us have difficulty remembering something. However, those with working memory deficits experience that occurrence regularly. Working memory is how we hold and save information we have learned so that we can access it when needed in the future. Working memory is vital for remembering steps to complete all tasks. As an adult with ADHD, I have discovered that my working memory is a significant deficit. However, using a variety of supports, I can be successful at my job, running my house, taking care of my children, and in graduate school as I work on my doctorate. I tell you this so you know that finding the appropriate support for essential life skills is essential to success in school and life.

Ways to teach and help your child with working memory:

THRIVE: Special Needs Strategies That WORK!

- Provide extra time.
- Use a reminder system such as a notebook, visuals, or a digital checklist.
- Allow a chance to redo unsuccessful assessments to demonstrate learning.
- Chunk assignments into small sections.
- Use repetition.
- Present information slowly and ensure understanding before moving forward.
- Use graphic organizers such as a note-taking template.

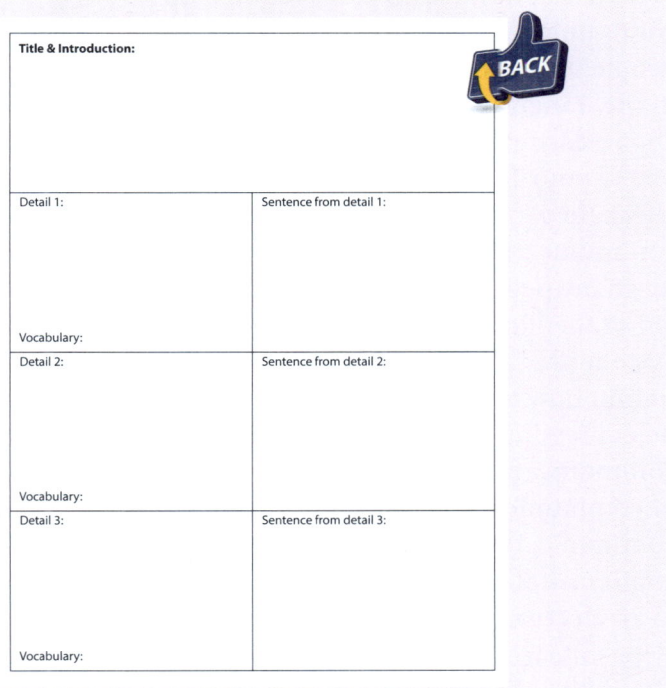

Figure 4.12. Another example of a graphic organizer that shows a child how to organize their writing for a writing prompt.

Sustained Attention

Sustained attention is the act of focusing on something and holding that focus over a period of time. Sustained attention is extremely important for a wide range of learning, including new skills, following instructions, engaging socially, and auditory processing, just to name a few. There are many factors that can affect sustained attention. Some of those factors include sensory considerations, learning diagnoses, and motivation.

Ways to teach and help a child with sustained attention:

- Use a timer.
- Shorten work tasks and provide frequent breaks.
- Give choices if motivation is a concern.
- Provide positive reinforcement when work is complete.
- Use first/then.
- Incorporate movement into activities and breaks.
- Teach self-management.

Task Initiation

Task initiation is beginning a task independently. Factors that influence task initiation include motivation, attention, and learning diagnoses. This is another essential skill for all people in all environments and seasons of life. People that struggle with task initiation may need multiple reminders to begin a task, try to escape from tasks, and engage in other activities such as drawing or asking to sharpen their pencil.

Ways to teach and help a child with task initiation:

- Self-management.
- Break tasks into steps — task analysis.
- Visual supports.
- An auditory or visual timer.
- Use a reinforcement system to motivate task initiation.

Basic Learning Skills

Communication

Communication is a foundational skill that everyone should be able to access. While communication is extremely difficult for some people, it is necessary for learning and engaging in life. I mention communication in this chapter about learning foundations because it should be one of your first steps for children needing an alternate communication method. Alternative communication can be extremely successful for many people. As a behavior analyst, I am a fan of the Picture Exchange Communication System (PECS) because the process of teaching a child how to use the system focuses not only on expressing themselves but getting their communication partner's attention, traveling to communicate, and being persistent with communication. Once a child knows how to communicate, the method can be transitioned to an electronic device. If a person knew the steps to teach those components with an alternative communication device, it would be possible to begin with a device instead of pictures, but the process is vital! However, I am not a trained professional in speech-language pathology, so I recommend that you seek information from a speech-language pathologist (SLP) for those components of communication.

I want to share a story about alternative communication from my days in the classroom. I had a student who was primarily non-vocal. He spoke in one- to two-word phrases for communication without support. At school, the student used pictures for communication. He would use the images to communicate in complete sentences with his pictures, but it was very limiting because he only had access to a specific number of images. I requested that he be transitioned from pictures to an electronic device for communication. I was denied because the student had spoken language, and the SLP feared it would stop him from gaining more vocal language. The following year, we had a different SLP, and she was on board with the plan of adding a portable electronic communication device. The day a device was brought into the classroom for him to trial, he navigated his way and found the words to tell us he was sad. He had never communicated about emotions until that point! I share this story for two reasons. The first is that if you feel a child's needs are not being met by one professional, seek out a second opinion. The second piece of advice is not to limit a child to speaking vocally because you are afraid they will not speak if they have something that speaks for them. PECS has been cited as useful in improving communication and not holding back the development of spoken communication.[20]

WRAP-UP

Teaching a child foundational learning skills is very important in setting the stage for learning that will serve them throughout life. Some of these skills will take a substantial amount of time to teach, but the time spent now will pay off. You are investing in a child's future!

May the God of hope fill you with all joy and peace in believing, so that by the power of the Holy Spirit you may abound in hope.

—Romans 15:13

5

Teaching Strategies

There is a quote by Walter Barbe[21] often said in the behavior analysis world: "If you've told a child a thousand times, and the child still has not learned, then it is not the child who is the slow learner." Another way you may have heard this sentiment is, "Insanity is doing the same thing over and over again, but expecting different results," spoken by Rita Mae Brown.[22]

I recently read a passage about the history of education. The passage shared that public education was shaped to prepare children for the most common workplace of the time: the factory. The workforce today is hugely different than the rigid workplace of the past. We are preparing children today for jobs that are not even created yet.

Perhaps this might seem like a bizarre way to begin a chapter about teaching. However, it often takes thinking "outside of the box" to help children with disabilities learn. All people can learn. Every. Single. Person. Sometimes it just takes different strategies than how we were taught as children. As an educator, you have the flexibility and autonomy to create any style of learning environment necessary to meet a child's needs. What a blessing!

In this chapter, we will review several strategies to support instruction as you teach new skills. This chapter is not an exhaustive list of teaching strategies. There are several that are best learned in person or with video modeling. This chapter on strategies to support teaching is important because it includes powerful tools that, when used correctly, can make a quick and impactful change in your daily life. A bonus is that many of these strategies can be used simultaneously. As with the other concepts in this book, they will take time and practice to become second nature. Choose one, practice, and give yourself grace as you learn new things.

Prompting

Prompting is an instructional strategy that supports students as they learn new skills. The goal of using a prompt is to get a student to the correct answer with as little intrusion as possible. The graphic to the right shows the types of prompts and gives a general flow of how they might work. However, it all depends on the student and the skill. If you research prompting, you will find many types of prompting hierarchies or flow charts and even different types of prompts. There isn't a one-stop shop for prompting, so the critical piece for you to know is the types of prompts and how they work together.

Figure 5.1. This visual shows an example of a prompting guide that could be used with a child for some skills.

Most Intrusive → Full Physical → Partial Physical → Verbal → Model → Gesture → Visuals → Natural Cue → Least Intrusive

Visuals can be used with all levels.

Let's dive deeper into the types of promptings. It will be essential to know how the different types interact as you learn to increase your prompt for incorrect responses and decrease your prompt for correct responses. As you can see on the graphic, visuals are appropriate for use across all prompting levels. You can also see the level of intrusiveness of the prompt and how dependent or independent the learner is based on the prompting hierarchy for that skill. Different skills could have different prompting paths. For example, if you ask for a verbal response, you cannot physically prompt a response. Therefore, those types of prompts would not be on the hierarchy for that skill.

Many workplaces now hang up visuals to support employees as they complete work tasks. Recently I was in a restaurant that sells tacos, and hanging at each station was a picture with instructions detailing how to make each type of taco. Some workers used the visuals, while others did not. For this example, we would consider the goal for the worker. Is the goal to fade the words and pictures to nothing? If the answer is yes, then it is a prompt. Is the goal to use the visuals independently? If the answer is yes, and they can use the visuals without other supports, then it would not be considered a prompt.

THRIVE: Special Needs Strategies That WORK!

Natural Cue

If a child can complete an activity or routine without support other than the same visuals everyone has, this would be considered independent. Many visuals support us daily on our cell phones, calendars, and other locations.

Example: The directions and other visuals on a worksheet the child will have.

Visuals

It would be considered a visual prompt if a child cannot complete an activity or routine without the visual.

Example: A visual task strip is needed to complete the handwashing routine.

Gesture

A gesture can be pointing, a head nod, an arm wave, or any body part used to express meaning or direction.

Example: You want a child to write their name on a piece of paper, so you point to the line that says, "Name."

Model

Modeling is completing the activity or direction the exact way you would like a child to do it while they watch.

Example: You want a child to rinse their dish in the sink, so you take your dish and show them exactly what to do.

Verbal

If a verbal direction is given as instructions for an activity, it is not considered a prompt in this scenario. If you must repeat the directions, it would then be regarded as a prompt. Any additional words the adult uses to provide direction above what the task calls for is a prompt. Many consider verbal prompts the most difficult to fade, especially for those who struggle with initiation. Each time a verbal reminder (prompt) is given to remind them to get started, it would be considered an additional prompt.

Example: It is time to put on pajamas before bedtime. You say, "Go put on your pajamas." The child continues engaging in their other activity. You again say, "Go put on your pajamas."

Partial Physical

Some activities require an adult to support a child by moving the child's arm toward an item or gently touching their elbow to get them started. This act would be considered a partial physical prompt because you physically touched them. Another example could be a gentle touch to the shoulder or placing a pencil in their hand with the correct grip.

Example: You ask a child to push in their chair. They do not, so you gently guide their elbow to place their hand on the back of the chair, and they do the rest.

Full Physical

Some consider full physical prompting to be the most intrusive type of prompt. I believe that is because someone is in the child's personal space and physically manipulating their body to complete the requested task. I cannot stress enough that you must not stay at this level any longer than absolutely necessary for the learner.

Example: It is dinner time. You recently began working on eating with a fork. The child just sits and looks at their plate. You take their hand with yours, help them pick up the fork, move the fork to the plate, stick the fork in the food, and bring the fork back to their mouth.

I love this example because we often do not think about how many steps there are to complete a simple task, such as taking a bite of food. If you have created a task analysis as discussed in Chapter 2, you would be able to note the prompt level of each step. Some children can perform some steps independently and only need support with a step or two. On the other hand, they may need maximum help for all steps, and the first time you can drop to a partial prompt on one step, you will be able to mark that growth!

Errorless Learning

Errorless learning happens when an adult provides the correct response via a prompt before the child responds to the request so that they only practice the correct answer. Ask the child to complete the task to determine what level of prompt to begin with and ensure they get the correct answer. Then start the process of fading out prompts until the child completes the task independently. If a child has difficulty learning the correct answer after completing the incorrect response several times, this would be a suitable prompting method to select.

General tips for prompting:

- Ensure you evaluate the child's progress as you follow your plan; if they stall, stop-drop-assess!
- Remember to reinforce heavily when children are even a tiny step more independent than they were before.
- Begin to fade prompts as quickly as possible. Some students will be able to fade the second time they try a skill, while others will need many trials. That is why data is so important. Most of us cannot remember the tiny details of each school day for multiple tasks and activities.
- To determine which level of prompting you should start, ask a child to complete the activity independently and see what they can do alone.

Fading Prompts

I have mentioned fading prompts several times, so now we are going to go more in-depth about the importance of successfully fading prompts, and I will share some tips on doing so. Prompts are not meant to be permanent. I have worked with many students in the past who were taught using prompts, but they were not faded. When this happens, children can become prompt-dependent. You will be able to spot these students because they will not attempt to complete the activity without adult support. I have seen children so prompt-dependent that when presented with directions, they placed their arm in the hand of the paraprofessional so they could move them through the motions of the task. Since our ultimate goal is independence, that is a big problem. We need to plan for fading from the beginning and fade prompts as soon as possible so your child does not become prompt-dependent.

Most to Least Prompt Fading

Most to least prompting is when you begin teaching the skills with the highest level of prompting. Most to least prompting is excellent for students who lack the necessary skills to complete a task. You would likely use this with children who have significant cognitive disabilities. A less intrusive prompt, such as guiding the learner at the wrist, is used for immediate additional attempts.

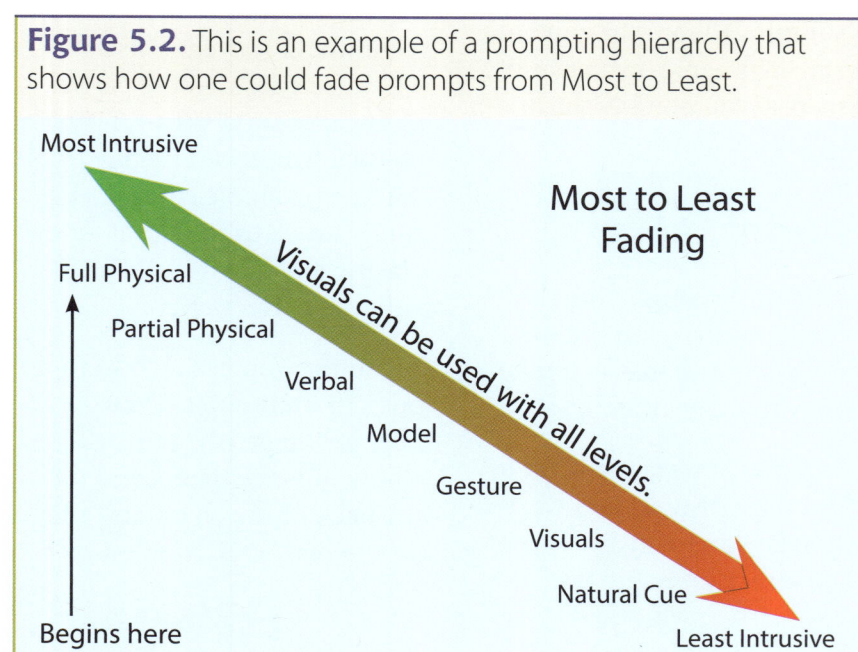

Figure 5.2. This is an example of a prompting hierarchy that shows how one could fade prompts from Most to Least.

Example: Flushing the toilet using most to least prompt fading:

- *Full Physical:* Use full physical assistance (hand under hand guidance) to fully assist the child in touching the handle and pushing it in the correct direction until the toilet flushes. (The full physical assistance prompt can be paired with the direct verbal prompt.)
- *Partial Physical:* Use physical assistance to help guide the child's hand to the lever but do not use full physical assistance to help the child complete the task of pushing the lever down to flush. (The partial physical assistance prompt can be paired with the direct verbal prompt.)
- *Verbal:* Tell the child, "Use your hand to push down the lever to flush." (The direct verbal prompt can be paired with the gesture or model prompt.)
- *Model:* Put your hand on the lever, push the lever down, and flush the toilet.
- *Gesture:* Direct the child to flush the toilet by pointing (gesturing) to the lever.
- *Visual:* Show the child an image/icon of a child flushing the toilet. (The visual prompt can be paired with the gesture prompt.)
- *Independent:* Take the child to the restroom. Once they finish using the bathroom, they flush independently.

Least to Most Prompting

When using least to most prompting, you would begin with the least amount of prompting necessary. As needed, more intrusive prompts are added for the student to complete the skill. Least to most prompting is excellent for students who have the prerequisite skills to complete the task but are not completing it.

Example: Cutting a circle outline on a paper.

- *Visual:* Show a picture or drawing of someone cutting a piece of paper.
- *Gesture:* Point to the scissors and the paper to indicate they should pick them up and begin.
- *Model:* You pick up the scissors and the paper and cut out the circle while they watch.
- *Verbal:* Ask the child to pick up the scissors, pick up the paper, and cut out the circle.
- *Partial Physical:* Support the child in putting their fingers in the scissors the correct way and support holding the paper with the other hand.
- *Full Physical:* The adult guides the child's hands in picking up the scissors and making the cutting motions while supporting the paper with the other hand.

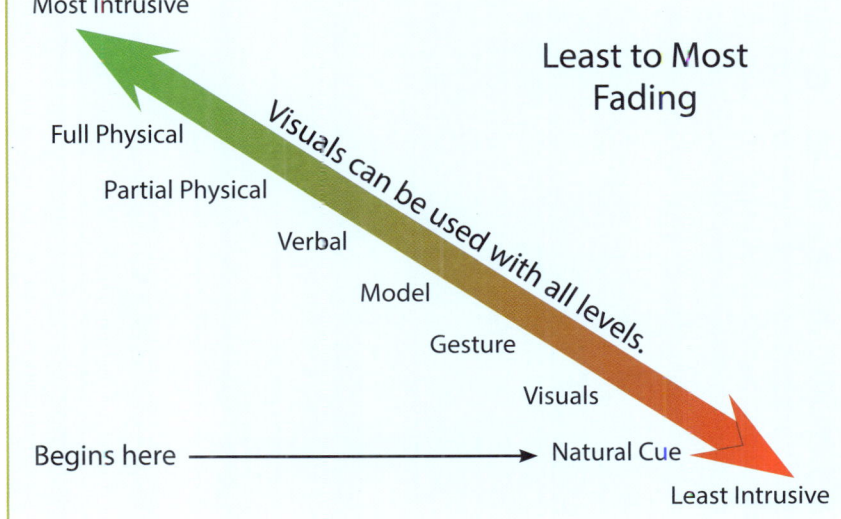

Figure 5.3. This example shows prompt fading in the form of least to most. While one would begin at the lowest form of a prompt to support the learner, they will then fade down to independence.

Teaching Strategies

Tips for fading prompts:

- Plan from the beginning what your prompt hierarchy will be. This will allow you to automatically know what prompt should be used next. For example, if you begin with a full physical prompt, your next step down would be a partial physical prompt. If you already have that planned out, you will be ready when the time comes.

- Break the task down into small steps (create a task analysis). This will allow you to note detailed information regarding prompt levels.

- Fade as quickly as possible. Do not wait to get comfortable. If you fade too soon, just put the higher level of support back in for the next attempt.

Accommodations

Accommodations are changes in how content is presented. They do not change expectations in performance or responsibilities. They simply change how a task is completed. Accommodations can be a presentation, response, setting, timing, or schedule changes. Below is a short list of potential accommodations that I used frequently with my students. A child could need accommodations in one content area and not others based on their strengths and growth areas.

Accommodation examples:

- Give verbal responses.
- Record the instructor to review again.
- Have another person read the content aloud.
- Listen to an audiobook instead of reading.
- Use a computer to type notes.
- Have a scribe write spoken responses.
- Access sensory items to support focus.
- Take frequent breaks when completing work.
- Highlight important text.
- Do oral testing to demonstrate knowledge.
- Give a choice of testing format.
- Use graphic organizers.

Modifications

Modifications change or reduce assignment content. They make the assignment easier than the grade level standard requires. Modifications are used for children who cannot comprehend their current grade level standards. It is possible that a child would need modifications in one content area and not others based on their strengths and growth areas.

Modification examples:

- Answering alternate questions than those in the lesson.
- Skipping specific content.
- Alternate vocabulary words.
- Word bank added to assignments.
- Using a different text.
- Removal of some learning standards.
- Reducing the expectations of assignments.
- Use a different grading scale.
- Prompting the student to the correct response.

THRIVE: Special Needs Strategies That WORK!

General Teaching Tips

In this section, I want to highlight some tips that encourage a good learning environment and instruction. These strategies support many different learners and are never a waste of time when incorporated into learning.

- *Clear one-step directions.* As adults, we tend to use too many words when giving directions. Use wording that is direct and to the point. If your child is ready for two-step directions or more, that is great. Go for it!

- *Pair oral instructions with visuals and writing.* Images and writing are great supports for learners. I encourage you to add these to your verbal presentation of directions.

- *Use manipulatives to support learning when possible.* Use hands-on items for lessons when possible. Hands-on items can provide a concrete connection for children as they learn and practice new information.

- *Wait time.* After you have presented instructions or new information, pause and give your child time to process that information. I recommend 2–3 minutes. It will seem like forever at first. However, providing time to process and organize the information they just received is vital. If sharing the new information, you could follow that wait time by asking if they would like to hear any of it again or have any questions.

- *Reduce distractions in the area if applicable (noise or items).* Remove distracting items or sounds if a child does best in a quiet or distraction-free learning environment. If removing a distracting sound is impossible, you could consider a white noise machine to drown out the other sound. However, some children will find the white noise machine distracting, so you must test what a child finds distracting.

- *Frequent breaks.* If a child has difficulty sitting or attending for long periods, consider taking short breaks every 15 minutes. Perhaps a child can focus for longer but needs longer breaks between content. That child could work longer but then receive an extended break time.

Individualized Engagement Strategies

- *Alternate seating.* As an individual with ADHD, comfort is significant for my working environment. I have chair cushions, fitness balls, wobble seats, and other seating options. I also sometimes work from my couch, bed, or floor. The seating location is not a critical part of the learning; the grasp of the content is! A quick internet search will lead you to many alternative seating options.

- *Movement breaks.* Allowing children to take a movement break between content or learning activities is an excellent method to enable them to get their "wiggles" out and regain focus for the next learning task. A few ideas could be dancing, a quick jog around the house, a brain break (search for these on the internet), or jumping jacks.

- *Listen to music while working.* Some children will find music calming and allow them to focus. This will not be the same for all children, but a quick test will be easy to complete. You can try different genres of music to see if any work better for focus than others. I often wear one earbud and listen to music on low while I am in meetings. This allows my brain to quiet and focus on the discussion. Those without ADHD may be unable to handle that much stimulation, but the key here is to try different strategies for a child.

- *Use interest for lessons.* If your curriculum allows, incorporate your child's interests into the lesson. Following a child's interest can make a huge difference in their engagement level in learning. This can be accomplished by selecting reading texts on their level about a topic of their interest. Another possibility is to use manipulatives of their interest. An example of this would be using dinosaur counters. The options for incorporating interests into learning are endless, so get creative!

WRAP-UP

This is not an all-inclusive list of teaching strategies. However, what I shared in this chapter will support any evidence-based teaching strategy. There are other strategies such as discrete trial training, pivotal response training, and functional communication training that are best learned through video modeling or another visual training method. If a child continues to struggle with instruction and the strategies in this book are not supporting their learning, keep trying!

For God gave us a spirit not of fear but of power and love and self-control.

—2 Timothy 1:7

And let us not grow weary of doing good, for in due season we will reap, if we do not give up.
— Galatians 6:9

As we end our time together, I want to congratulate you on a job well done. I am not in the room while you teach, but I know from past experience that teaching is often challenging and thankless. Many of the most important lessons we learn as teachers are found in tough scenarios. Reflecting on those tough times can instill in us lessons that will help us improve our instruction and be used in many scenarios throughout our lives. Be kind to yourself as you learn new strategies and practice implementing them. Every mistake can lead to the refinement of your new skills. Mistakes are how many of us learn! It took me a long time to embrace that concept, but it has been life-changing.

Galatians 6:9 says, "And let us not grow weary of doing good, for in due season we will reap, if we do not give up." This promise is to remind you that your devotion to a child's learning and education is not in vain. Your dedication to providing a child with exactly what they need is inspiring to me! You've got this!

This book has many strategies and resources that can be individualized for any student. I often tell teachers, "A good teaching strategy is a good teaching strategy." If you are not seeing growth with a strategy, do some investigating! Often we are missing one little component that, once discovered and adjusted, can make all the difference! If it works for you in the home setting, why limit its value? I suggest you try it in multiple settings if needed, such as at a store, church, restaurant, and anywhere your child goes!

>  **Pro tip:** There are a lot of strategies in this book, and perhaps you are feeling overwhelmed. I suggest you choose one strategy and start there. Get comfortable with it, and then select another one. Give yourself and a child time to get used to a strategy before adding more.

I believe every child is unique and special, with specific strengths and needs. I believe that every child can learn. The pace and outcomes will vary, but we are all capable of growth. I'm so thankful God created us to be unique. Each one of us can be used by God for His purposes, and I believe this especially includes children with disabilities. I have learned so much beyond education from my former students. They leave a positive impact on my life long after we part ways.

In America, we are inundated with images and words of what we should be, what our families should be like, and so on and so forth. Children with special needs do not often fit in those cookie-cutter molds we are sold by advertisers. Don't settle for those images. I hope you end this book feeling encouraged that you CAN create the environment and be the support a child needs to succeed in school and life. Keep trying new strategies until you find what works for a child. It's okay if it isn't what you expected. Do not be afraid of thinking outside of the box. You will find what works.

Take this journey one step at a time and remember, God created you for such a time as this!

Glossary

Accommodations: These are changes in how content is presented.

Errorless learning: This happens when an adult provides the correct response via a prompt before the child responds to the request.

Fidget: Can be anything that a person uses to engage in motor movements while at the same time engaging in their current activity.

Icon schedules: Uses images that represent activities, items, and locations that a child needs to navigate through the day.

Landing zone: This is where a child will place their object or icon when they complete the given task or activity.

Mini schedules: Visual supports broken down into smaller steps than what they see on their visual schedule.

Motor/object imitation: This is copying a motor movement after watching another person complete it.

Object schedules: A type of visual schedule where you select objects representing activities or locations the child will need throughout their day. They are beneficial for children not yet communicating with words or signs.

Photograph schedules: Created by taking photographs of exact locations, activities, or items used for a child's daily schedule.

Positive reinforcement: When you provide a child with a reinforcer (an item THEY desire) after the child gives the response YOU want.

Prompting: This is an instructional strategy that supports students as they learn new skills.

Reinforcement: Defined as having a child do one task then providing them with one item or activity for reinforcement.

Reinforcers: These reinforcements can be any item, food, social interaction, or activity.

Self-management: Teaching a child to manage their behavior.

Social narratives (stories): To create a social story, we take a problem and provide alternative behaviors we would like to see.

Sustained attention: This is the act of focusing on something and holding that focus over a period of time.

Task analysis: Made by breaking an activity into smaller, more manageable steps, so the child knows each step and the correct order needed to complete an activity.

Task initiation: This is beginning a task independently.

Token economy: Tokens are earned and traded for a reinforcer.

Visual schedules: A type of visual support that provides structure and help a child navigate their day.

Visual supports: These are images paired with verbal instructions that support the comprehension of spoken word(s).

Words-only schedule: Shows the order of activities the child will complete throughout the day.

Words with icons schedule: Created using images representing activities and locations that a child needs to navigate through the day.

Working memory: This is how we hold and save information we have learned so that we can access it when needed in the future.

Index

Accommodations 78, 83
Autism 36, 56
Behavior ...9, 11, 15, 20, 23, 25, 27, 31, 33, 37-38, 45-46, 48-50, 52, 56, 59, 72-73, 83
Break 12, 14, 20-21, 50, 52, 67-68, 71, 78-79
Challenging behavior 20, 23, 25, 27, 31, 33, 37, 46, 48-50, 52
Change 6, 20-21, 23, 36-37, 40, 53, 61, 74, 78
Choice board 11, 20
Communication 25, 37, 56, 72, 80
Container method 17-18
Conversation visuals 58
Coping strategies 56
Cue to transition 40
Data collection sheet 44
Datasheet 11, 48-49, 59, 65, 89-90
Emotional control 69
Emotional skills 55
Emotions 55-56, 69, 72
Errorless learning 76, 83
Fading prompts 40, 76, 78
Fidgets 21
Follow through 10
Gesture 75, 77
Icon 27, 29-30, 37, 39-42, 50, 52, 77, 83
Icon schedules 27, 29, 83
Independence 5, 7, 23-24, 39, 55, 62, 64, 76
Labels 29, 45, 55
Lamination 35, 47, 89-90
Landing zone 40-42, 83
Life skills 5, 23, 37, 44, 64, 67, 69-70
Loop 15, 35
Mini schedule 32-33
Modeling 54, 63, 74-75, 80

Modifications 78
Motor 21, 62-63, 83
Neutral 17, 36-37, 46
Object schedules 25, 83
One-step directions 63-64, 79
Open hand method 17
Organization 8, 34-35, 64, 68
Photograph schedules 26-27, 83
Physical limitations 32
Positive reinforcement .. 7-9, 11-12, 19-20, 22, 54, 71, 83
Positive Reinforcement Checklist 20, 131
Printing 35, 53
Promise procedure 18
Prompting 39, 46, 50, 64-65, 74-78, 83
Reinforcer 8, 11-12, 18-20, 83
Routines 32, 55, 62, 64-65, 68
Self-management 23-24, 37-38, 71, 83
Skill ... 9, 21, 32, 36-38, 42, 52, 55, 62-64, 68, 71-72, 74, 76-77
Social narratives 56, 83
Special .. 3-5, 7, 19, 21-22, 32, 35-36, 39, 44, 62, 67, 82, 85-86, 113
Storage 34-35
Structure 7-8, 21-23, 33, 44, 64, 84
Structured learning environment 21
Sustained attention 71, 83
Task analysis .. 24, 32-33, 42, 65, 68, 71, 75, 78, 83, 141
Task initiation 71, 83
Time ... 6, 9, 11-12, 15, 17-24, 33, 36-40, 42, 44, 48-50, 53-54, 59-61, 65, 68, 71-76, 78-79, 81-83
Time management 68
Timers 22, 39, 53, 68
Token board 12, 14, 65, 143
Token economy 12, 83
Transition strategies 39

Velcro 6, 19-20, 35, 47, 89-90
Video modeling 54, 74, 80
Visual........11-12, 17, 21-25, 27, 32-37, 39-40, 42-46, 48-50, 52-56, 58-60, 64-65, 68, 71, 75, 77, 80, 83
Visual model 33
Visual schedules.......... 11, 22-24, 35-37, 39, 42, 44, 84

Visual support................... 11, 23, 32, 48, 50, 52-53, 84
Visual timer.......................... 17, 39, 49, 53, 71
Words-only schedule..31, 84
Words with icons schedule...................................30, 84
Working memory 70, 84

Endnotes

Introduction

1. www.andyhargreaves.com/grants.html.

Chapter 1

2. S. Kucharczyk, *Reinforcement (R+) Fact Sheet* (Chapel Hill, NC: The University of North Carolina, Frank Porter Graham Child Development Institute, The National Professional Development Center on Autism Spectrum Disorders, 2013).
3. J.O. Cooper, T.E. Heron, and W.L. Heward, *Applied Behavior Analysis,* 3rd Edition, "Positive Reinforcement" (Hoboken, NJ: Pearson Education, 2019).
4. Kucharczyk, *Reinforcement (R+) Fact Sheet.*

Chapter 2

5. L. Bryan and D. Gast, *Journal of Autism and Developmental Disorders*, "Teaching On-Task and On-Schedule Behaviors to High-Functioning Children with Autism Via Picture Activity Schedules, 2000, p. 553–567, http://dx.doi.org/10.1023/A:1005687310346.
6. K.A. Quill, ed., *Teaching Children with Autism: Strategies to Enhance Communication and Socialization,* L.Q. Hodgdon, "Solving Social-Behavioral Problems Through the Use of Visually Supported Communication," p. 265–286 (New York: Delmar, 1995).
7. K. Hume and S. Smith, *Steps for Implementation: Visual Schedules* (Chapel Hill, NC: National Professional Development Center on Autism Spectrum Disorders, Frank Porter Graham Child Development Institute, The University of North Carolina, 2009), retrieved June 2, 2021, from https://autismpdc.fpg.unc.edu/sites/autismpdc.fpg.unc.edu/files/imce/documents/VisualSupports_Complete.pdf.
8. Ibid.
9. Ibid.
10. Ibid.
11. M.E. Brock, *Self-Management (SM) Fact Sheet* (Chapel Hill, NC: National Professional Development Center on Autism Spectrum Disorders, Frank Porter Graham Child Development Institute, The University of North Carolina, 2013), retrieved June 2, 2021, from https://autismpdc.fpg.unc.edu/sites/autismpdc.fpg.unc.edu/files/SelfManagement_factsheet.pdf.
12. Earles, T. L., Carlson, J. K., & Bock, S. J. (1998). Instructional strategies to facilitate successful learning outcomes for students with autism. In R. L. Simpson & B. S. Myles (Eds.), Educating children and youth with autism: Strategies for effective practice (pp. 55–111). Austin: PRO-ED.
13. Hume and Smith, *Steps for Implementation: Visual Schedules.*
14. Ibid.

Chapter 3

15. K. Hume and S. Smith, *Steps for Implementation: Visual Supports* (Chapel Hill, NC: National Professional Development Center on Autism Spectrum Disorders, Frank Porter Graham Child Development Institute, The University of North Carolina, 2009), retrieved January 4, 2022, from https://autismpdc.fpg.unc.edu/sites/autismpdc.fpg.unc.edu/files/imce/documents/VisualSupports_Complete.pdf.
16. S. Smith and L. Collet-Klingenberg, *Steps for Implementation: Visual Boundaries* (Madison, WI: The National Professional Development Center on Autism Spectrum Disorders, Waisman Center, University of Wisconsin, 2009), retrieved January 4, 2022, from https://autismpdc.fpg.unc.edu/sites/autismpdc.fpg.unc.edu/files/imce/documents/VisualSupports_Complete.pdf.
17. C. Wong, *Social Narratives (SN) Fact Sheet* (Chapel Hill: The University of North Carolina, Frank Porter Graham Child Development Institute, The National Professional Development Center on Autism Spectrum Disorders, 2013), retrieved January 4, 2022, from https://autismpdc.fpg.unc.edu/sites/autismpdc.fpg.unc.edu/files/SocialNarratives_factsheet.pdf.

Chapter 4

18. J. Kohyama, "Good Daily Habits During the Early Stages of Life Determine Success Throughout Life," *Sleep Science,* 9(3), 2016, p. 153–157, https://10.1016/j.slsci.2016.09.002.
19. Silvana M.R. Watson, Robert A. Gable, and Lisa L. Morin, "The Role of Executive Functions in Classroom Instruction of Students with Learning Disabilities," *Communication Disorders & Special Education Faculty Publications,* 14 (Old Dominion University, 2016), https://digitalcommons.odu.edu/cdse_pubs/14.
20. L. Schreibman and A.C. Stahmer, (2014). "A Randomized Trial Comparison of the Effects of Verbal and Pictorial Naturalistic Communication Strategies on Spoken Language for Young Children with Autism," *Journal of Autism and Developmental Disorders*, May 2014, https://doi.org/10.1007/s10803-013-1972-y.

Chapter 5

21. Walter Barbe commented in an in-service workshop address (Marshall University, 1977).
22. Rita Mae Brown, *Sudden Death* (New York: Bantam Books, 1983), p. 68.

Datasheets & Manipulatives

Datasheets and manipulatives are invaluable tools that unlock the door to interactive and engaging learning experiences, especially for students with special needs. In this section, we delve into the fascinating realm of manipulatives, exploring how simple yet ingenious resources like Velcro and lamination can make a world of difference in the education of exceptional learners.

Manipulatives are tactile and visual aids that transform abstract concepts into concrete, hands-on experiences. They serve as bridges between ideas and understanding, helping students grasp complex subjects in a way that traditional methods often cannot.

With its hook-and-loop design, Velcro enables the creation of interactive boards, schedules, and activities that can be customized to suit individual learning needs. Its tactile nature makes it ideal for learners who benefit from sensory stimulation and tactile feedback. Whether it's creating storyboards, teaching math concepts, or developing communication tools, Velcro brings learning to life through touch.

Lamination, on the other hand, offers durability and reusability. By preserving resources like flashcards, visual aids, and communication boards under a protective layer, educators can extend the lifespan of these materials, saving both time and resources. Laminated materials are also easy to clean and maintain, making them suitable for various learning environments.

In the pages ahead, you'll find innovative ways to incorporate Velcro, lamination, and other tools into your teaching strategies, providing endless possibilities to enhance the educational journey of your special needs students with sheets mentioned throughout the book.

Datasheets and Manipulatives

Consumable Supply List

Note: All items will only be needed if every suggestion in the book is implemented.

- ☐ Paper
- ☐ Cardstock
- ☐ Velcro
- ☐ Scissors
- ☐ Dry-erase marker
- ☐ Expo marker
- ☐ Lamination sheets
- ☐ Construction paper
- ☐ Writing utensil
- ☐ Schedule and transition objects
- ☐ Clipboard
- ☐ Tape
- ☐ Glue sticks
- ☐ Items or images for tokens
- ☐ Posterboard
- ☐ Binder
- ☐ Binder rings
- ☐ Craft foam sheets
- ☐ Storage for images or objects
- ☐ Container or envelope for transition items or pictures
- ☐ Fabric
- ☐ Brads
- ☐ Simple objects
- ☐ Organizing materials
- ☐ Items to create structure
- ☐ Envelope
- ☐ Transition object

Equipment/Software List

Note: All items will only be needed if every suggestion in the book is implemented.

- ☐ Printer or print service
- ☐ Computer
- ☐ Computer word processing program (Docs, Slides, Word, or professional program)
- ☐ Laminator
- ☐ Camera or phone camera
- ☐ Hot glue gun
- ☐ Dry-erase board
- ☐ Timer
- ☐ Label maker
- ☐ Zipper pouch
- ☐ Digital programs for icons: There are several programs available for purchase at varying price points if you would like uniform icons. You can search the internet for "icon program for special needs" or a similar phrase to find various programs.
- ☐ Scissors

Datasheets & Manipulatives Table of Contents

The following perforated pages contain various datasheets and manipulatives that were mentioned throughout this book. The first pages contain various tokens that can be laminated, cut, and affixed to Velcro so that you can reuse them with the datasheets as often as you need. Sort them by size and topic in several envelopes.

Please know that permission is granted for copies of these reproducible pages from the text to be made for use only with your immediate family members who are living in the same household. Note that some figures use more than one kind of token.

Datasheet	Small Token	Large Token	Long Token	No Token
Figure 1.1 p133	Figure 1.2 p147	Figure 1.3 p149	Figure 1.3 p149	Figure 2.13 p165
Figure 1.12 p135	Figure 1.3 p149	Figure 1.9 p151	Figure 2.6 p155	Figure 3.31 p185
Figure 2.24 p137	Figure 2.4 p153	Figure 2.17 p167	Figure 2.9 p159	Figure 4.8 p201
Figure 2.26 p139	Figure 2.5 p153	Figure 2.19 p171	Figure 2.11 p163	Figure 4.11 p205
Figure 2.32 p141	Figure 2.8 p157	Figure 3.1 p175	Figure 3.32 p187	Figure 4.12 p207
Figure 3.6 p143	Figure 2.9 p159	Figure 3.5 p177	Figure 4.2 p191	
Figure 3.33 p145	Figure 2.10 p161	Figure 3.12 p179		
	Figure 2.11 p163	Figure 3.26 p181		
	Figure 2.18 p169	Figure 3.30 p183		
	Figure 2.25 p173	Figure 4.10 p203		
	Figure 4.1 p189			
	Figure 4.2 p191			
	Figure 4.3 p193			
	Figure 4.4 p195			
	Figure 4.5 p197			
	Figure 4.6 p199			

Figure 1.3 on page 149 can use any size token.

Datasheets and Manipulatives

Page intentionally left blank.

Small Tokens for Figures 1.2 through 2.8

Page is blank for cutting purposes.

Small Tokens for Figures 2.8 through 2.25

Page is blank for cutting purposes.

Small Tokens for Figures 2.25 through 4.2

Page is blank for cutting purposes.

Small Tokens for Figures 4.2 through 4.6 (with extra food tokens)

Page is blank for cutting purposes.

Blank Small Tokens

Page is blank for cutting purposes.

Large Tokens for Figures 1.9 through Teeth Brushing Lesson (Chapter 2)

Page is blank for cutting purposes.

Large Tokens for Teeth Brushing Lesson through Figure 2.17

Page is blank for cutting purposes.

Large Tokens for Figure 2.17 through Figure 3.4

Page is blank for cutting purposes.

Large Tokens for Figure 3.5 through Figure 3.13

Page is blank for cutting purposes.

Large Tokens for Figure 3.14 through Figure 3.26

Page is blank for cutting purposes.

Large Tokens for Figure 3.27 through Figure 3.30

Page is blank for cutting purposes.

Large Tokens for Figure 3.30 through Figure 4.10 (with Extra Activity Tokens)

Page is blank for cutting purposes.

Extra Large Tokens of Games and Special Activities

Page is blank for cutting purposes.

Extra Large Tokens of Food and Drink

Page is blank for cutting purposes.

Blank Large Tokens

Page is blank for cutting purposes.

Breakfast	Math
Work Table	Lunch
Put clothes in hamper	Exercise
Work Table	Science
Lunch	Breakfast
Work Table	Chores
Clean up toys	Reading
Breakfast	Exercise
Reading	Lunch
Chores	Math

Long Tokens for Figure 2.6 through Figure 2.11

Page is blank for cutting purposes.

Read	Bathtub
Chores	Wall
Math	Couch
Lunch	Window
Recess/Free Time	Door
Write	Off
Table	Sink
Chair	TV
Computer	Picture
On	Bed

Long Tokens for Figure 2.12 through Figure 3.24

Page is blank for cutting purposes.

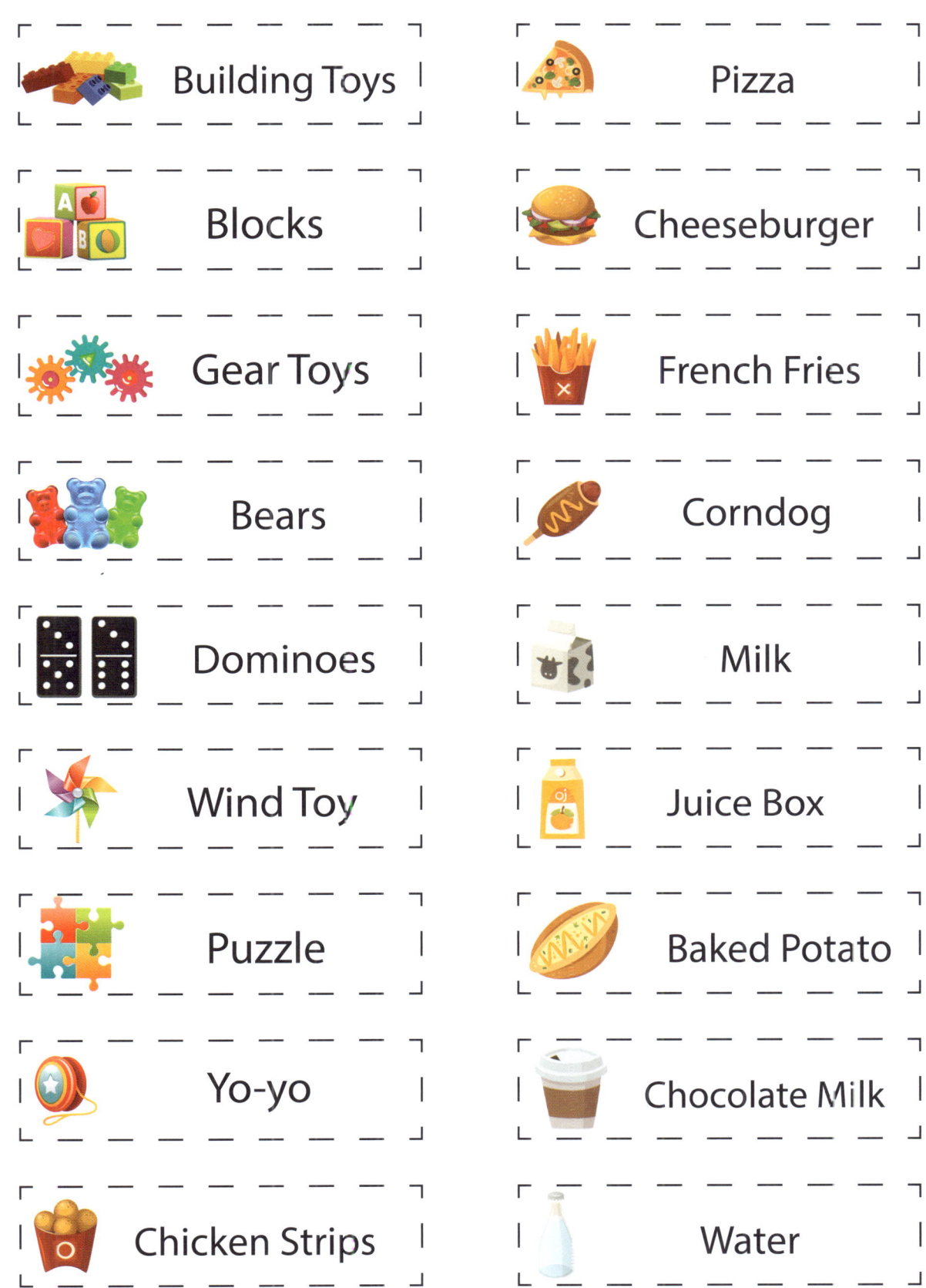

Long Tokens for Figure 3.25 through Figure 3.32

Page is blank for cutting purposes.

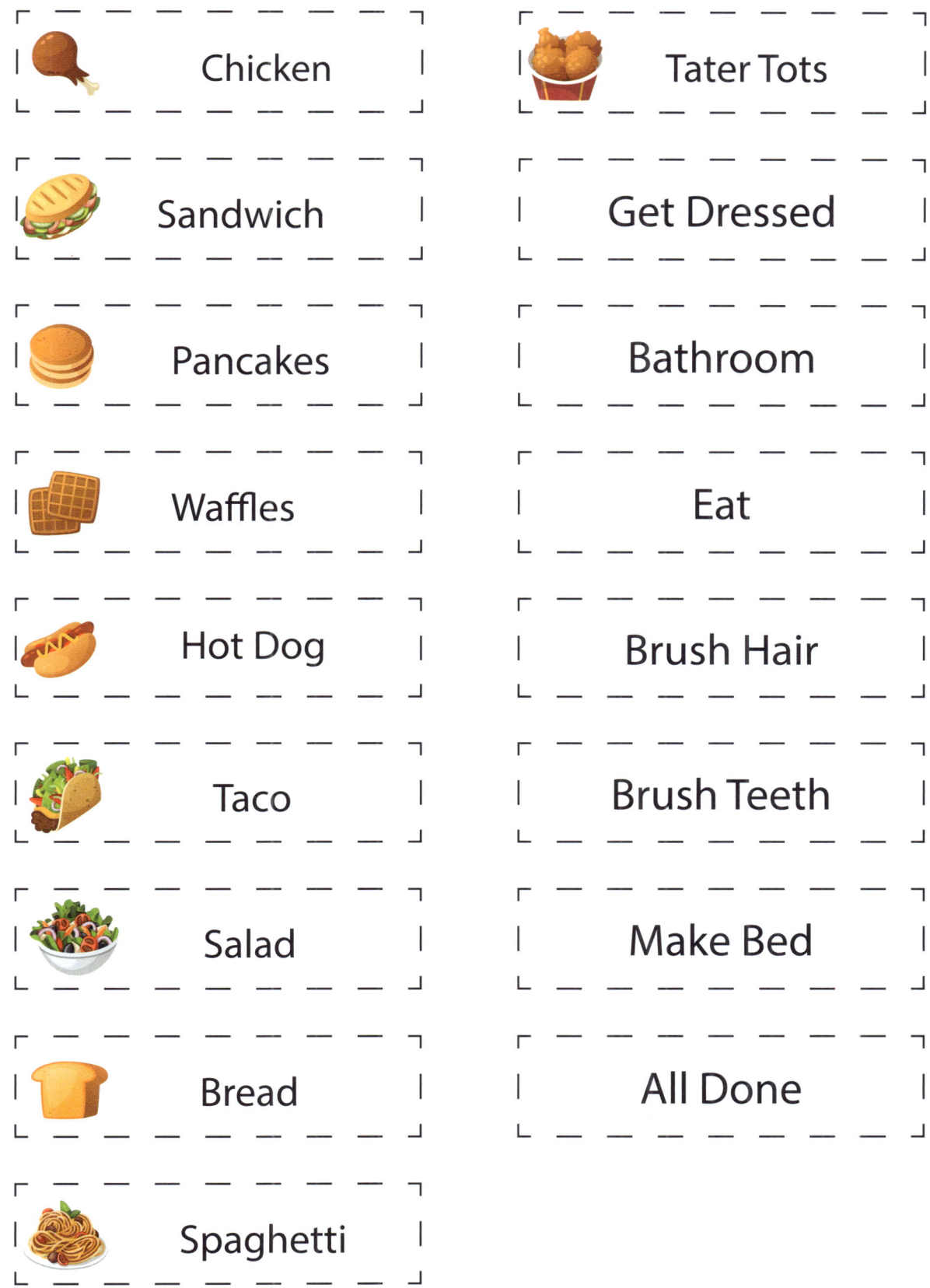

Long Tokens for Figure 3.32 through Figure 4.2

Page is blank for cutting purposes.

Blank Long Tokens (Labels)

Page is blank for cutting purposes.

Datasheet by Opportunity

Name: _____ Skill targeted: _____

Directions: For each opportunity the targeted skill is presented to the child, mark a (___) for correct responses. Mark a (___) for incorrect responses. *Example: + for correct, – for incorrect.*

Date	1	2	3	4	5	6	7	8	9	10	Notes

Figure 1.1

Page intentionally left blank.

Positive Reinforcement Checklist

This checklist can be printed out and used to ensure that all of the steps necessary for successfully using positive reinforcement are in place. Troubleshooting hints are located on page 20.

1. ☐ Let the child choose the item they are working toward (verbal, gesture, visual).

2. ☐ Present your demand.

3. ☐ Give the child adequate time to complete the task.

4. ☐ Present the child with the reinforcer they selected.

5. ☐ Set a timer to signal the end of reinforcement time.

Figure 1.12

Page intentionally left blank.

	Reading		Chores		Math		Writing		Science		Total Points
	Student	Adult	Student	Adult	Student	Adult	Student	Adult	Student	Adult	
________	+ −	+ −	+ −	+ −	+ −	+ −	+ −	+ −	+ −	+ −	
________	+ −	+ −	+ −	+ −	+ −	+ −	+ −	+ −	+ −	+ −	
Points											

Figure 2.24 0 points if no match 1 point if the adult scores a + 2 points if both score a +

	Reading		Chores		Math		Writing		Science		Total Points
	Student	Adult	Student	Adult	Student	Adult	Student	Adult	Student	Adult	
________	+ −	+ −	+ −	+ −	+ −	+ −	+ −	+ −	+ −	+ −	
________	+ −	+ −	+ −	+ −	+ −	+ −	+ −	+ −	+ −	+ −	
Points											

Figure 2.24 0 points if no match 1 point if the adult scores a + 2 points if both score a +

Page intentionally left blank.

Daily Behavior Tracker

	Yes	No
	Yes	No
	Yes	No
	Yes	No
	Yes	No
	Yes	No
	Yes	No
	Yes	No
	Yes	No

Figure 2.26

Page intentionally left blank.

Task Analysis

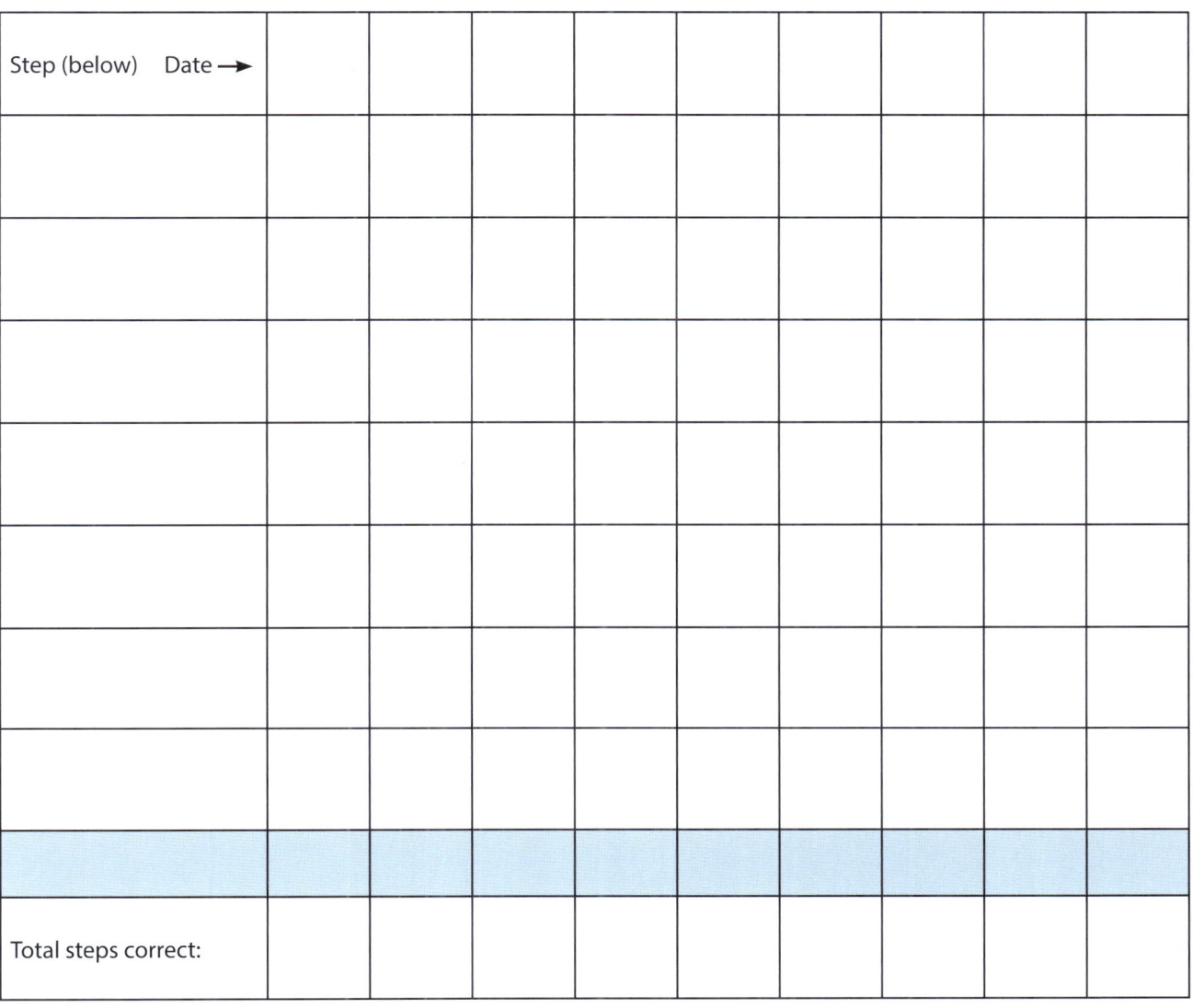

Y – Independent

N – Not independent (also indicate prompt level used)

FP – Full Physical

PP – Partial Physical

VB – Verbal

M – Model

G – Gesture

VI – Visual

Figure 2.32

Page intentionally left blank.

Wait Datasheet

Date	Trial	Item Student Wanted	Wait Time	# of Times Needed to Count	Challenging Behavior Observed

Figure 3.6

Page intentionally left blank.

Partial Interval Datasheet

Date: _____   Length of each observation interval: _____

Behavior you are targeting (it must be observable and measurable, define it very specifically).

_____
_____
_____

	Interval										Total (+)s
	1	2	3	4	5	6	7	8	9	10	
+ or −											

	Interval										Total (+)s
	1	2	3	4	5	6	7	8	9	10	
+ or −											

	Interval										Total (+)s
	1	2	3	4	5	6	7	8	9	10	
+ or −											

	Interval										Total (+)s
	1	2	3	4	5	6	7	8	9	10	
+ or −											

	Interval										Total (+)s
	1	2	3	4	5	6	7	8	9	10	
+ or −											

Figure 3.33

Page intentionally left blank.

10 Token Board

I am working for:

Figure 1.2

Page intentionally left blank.

I am working for:

Figure 1.3

Page intentionally left blank.

Break Choices

Figure 1.9

Page intentionally left blank.

Figure 2.4

1st

2nd

3rd

4th

5th

6th

7th

Figure 2.5

Page intentionally left blank.

_____'s Schedule

Figure 2.6

Page intentionally left blank.

Figure 2.8

Page intentionally left blank.

Weekday Schedule

Figure 2.9

Page intentionally left blank.

Figure 2.10

_____'s Schedule

Page intentionally left blank.

_____'s Schedule

Today is _____

Figure 2.11

Page intentionally left blank.

_____'s Schedule

Today is _____

Activity	Check for Completed
_____	_____
_____	_____
_____	_____
_____	_____
_____	_____
_____	_____

Figure 2.13

Page intentionally left blank.

Figure 2.17

Page intentionally left blank.

Using the Bathroom

☐	Walk to the bathroom	☐	Pants Down
☐	Pull Underwear Down	☐	Go to the Bathroom
☐	Get Toilet Paper	☐	Wipe
☐	Put Dirty Paper in the Toilet	☐	Flush
☐	Pull Underwear Up	☐	Pants Up

Figure 2.18

Page intentionally left blank.

Cleaning Up Toys

Figure 2.19

Cleaning Up Toys

Figure 2.19

Page intentionally left blank.

_____'s Schedule/Tracker

Figure 2.25

Page intentionally left blank.

First	Then

Figure 3.1

©Master Books 2023. All rights reserved.

First	Then

Figure 3.1

©Master Books 2023. All rights reserved.

Page is blank for cutting purposes.

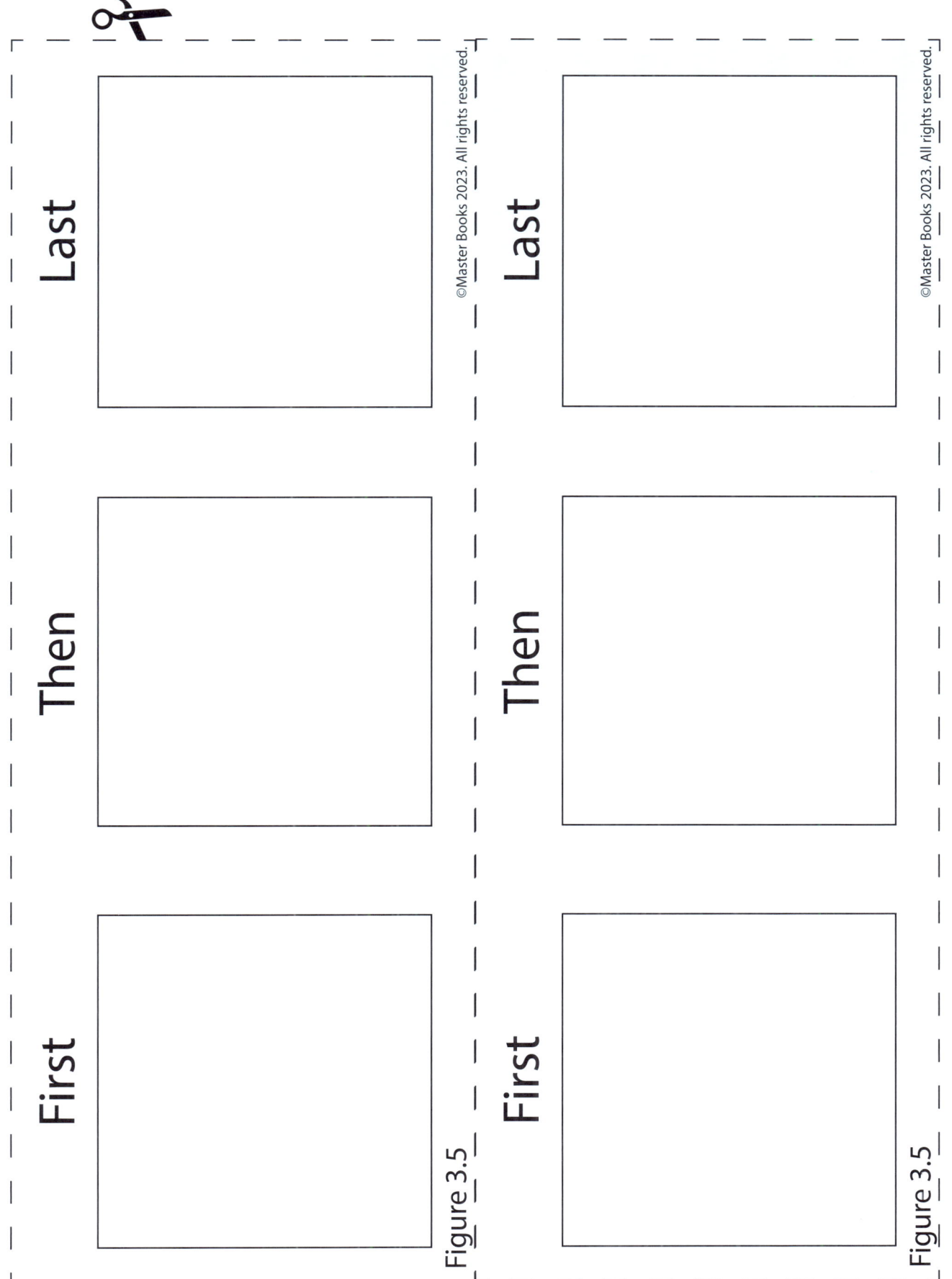

Page intentionally left blank.

I Need a Break

Figure 3.12

Page intentionally left blank.

Figure 3.26

Page is blank for cutting purposes.

Figure 3.30

Page is blank for cutting purposes.

Stay On Topic

Game

Figure 3.31

Page intentionally left blank.

Menu Card Keychain

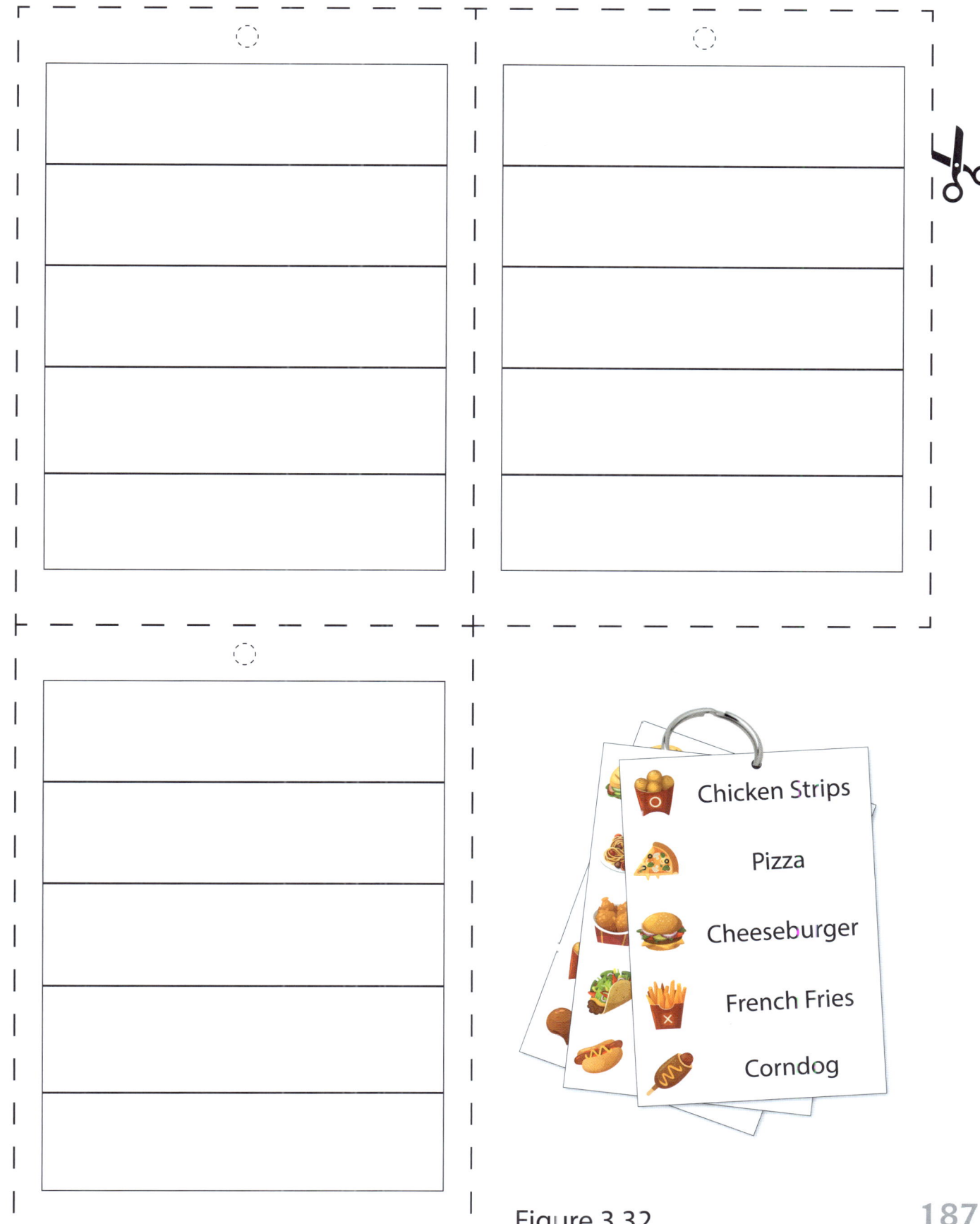

Figure 3.32

Page is blank for cutting purposes.

Picking Up Dirty Clothes

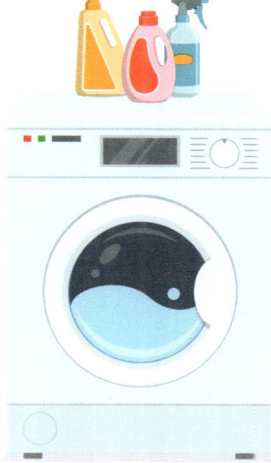

☐ Pick up dirty clothes

☐ Walk to hamper

☐ Put clothes in hamper

☐ Close closet door

Figure 4.1

Page intentionally left blank.

Morning To-Do List

Figure 4.2

Page intentionally left blank.

Figure 4.3

Page intentionally left blank.

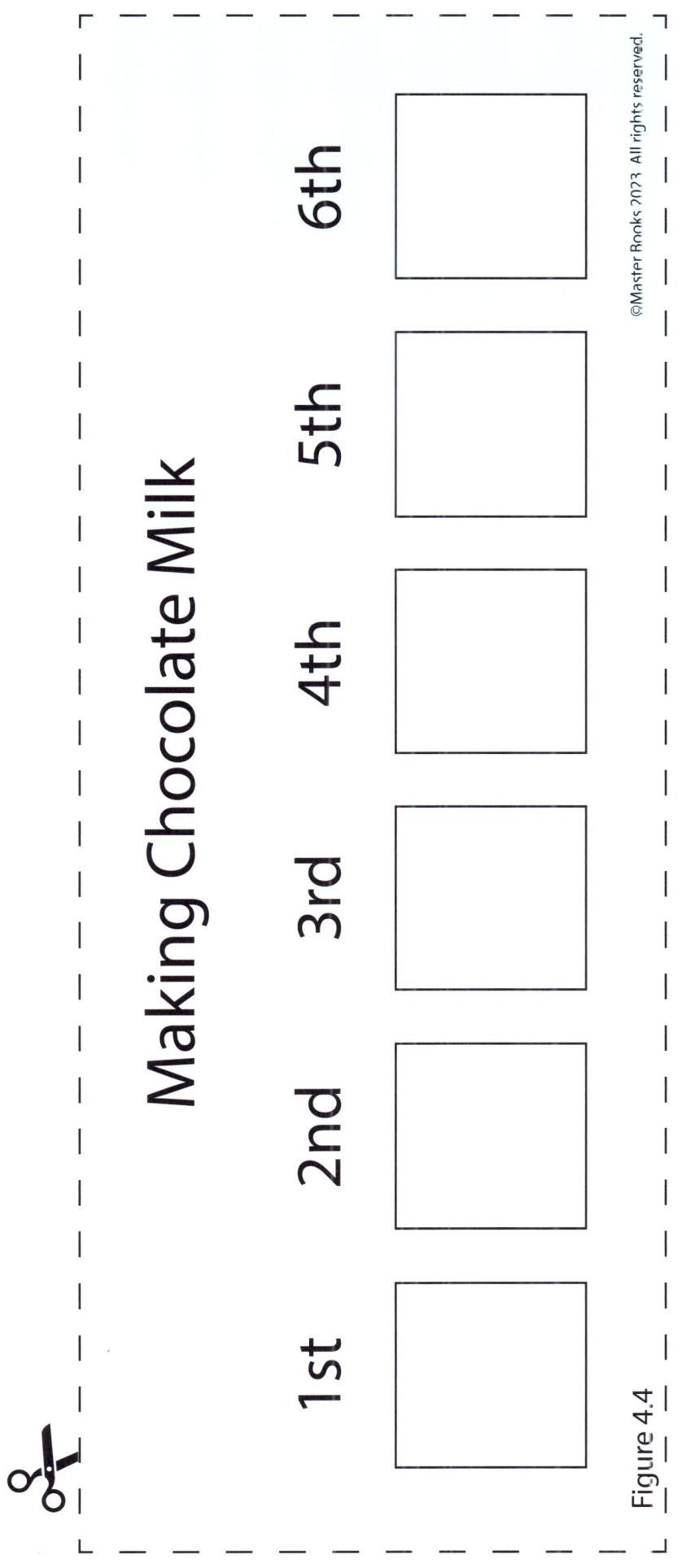

Figure 4.4

Page is blank for cutting purposes.

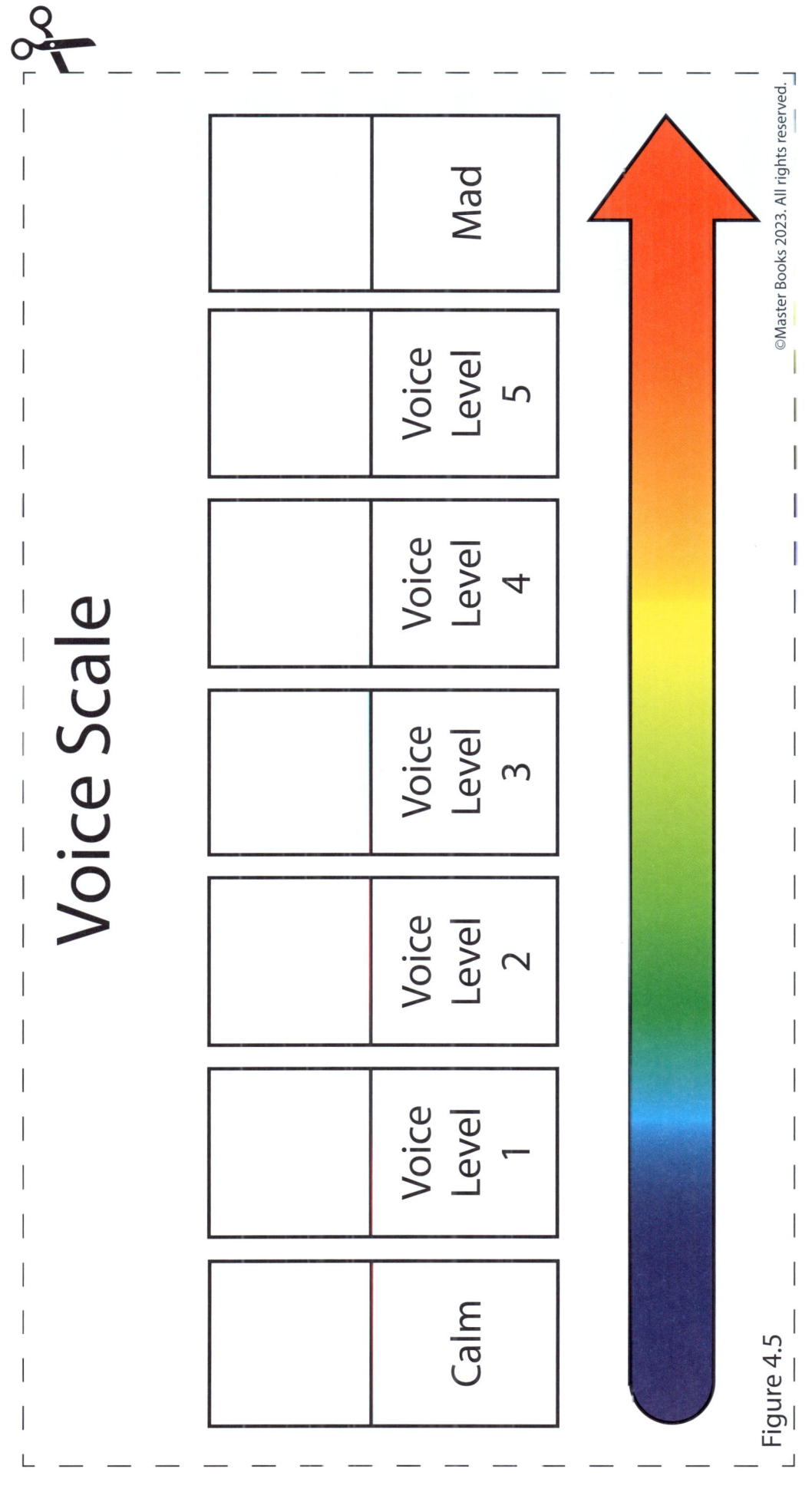

Figure 4.5

Page is blank for cutting purposes.

Figure 4.6

Page intentionally left blank.

Voice Scale

5	😊 Happy
4	🙂 Nervous
3	😐 Upset
2	🙁 Frustrated
1	☹️ Angry

Figure 4.8

©Master Books 2023. All rights reserved.

Page is blank for cutting purposes.

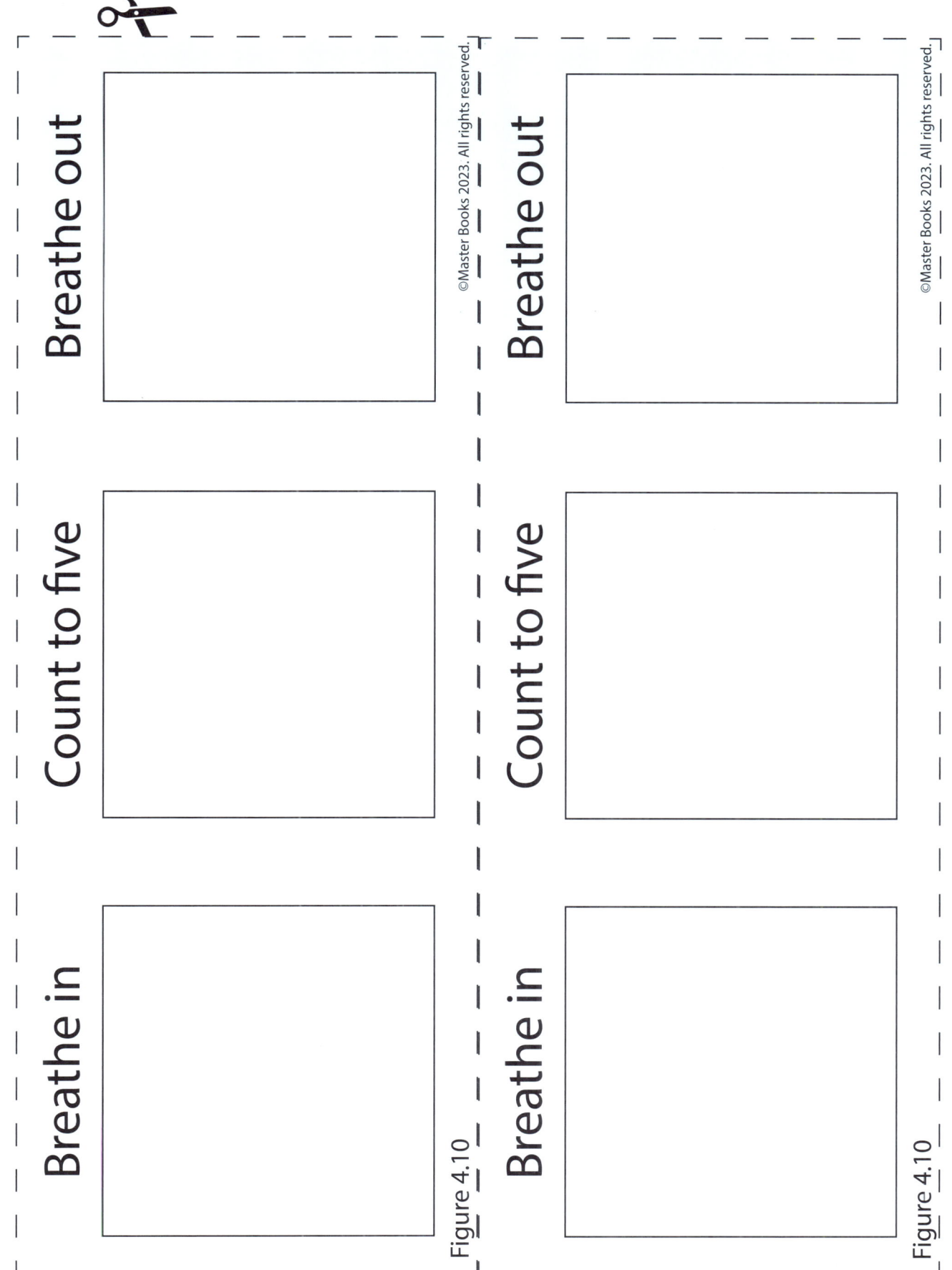

Figure 4.10

Page intentionally left blank.

TITLE:	
Main Idea: Vocabulary:	Characters:
Setting(s):	Questions I have:

Figure 4.11

Page intentionally left blank.

Title & Introduction:	
Detail 1: Vocabulary:	Sentence from detail 1:
Detail 2: Vocabulary:	Sentence from detail 2:
Detail 3: Vocabulary:	Sentence from detail 3:

Figure 4.12

Page intentionally left blank.

The steadfast love of the LORD never ceases; his mercies never come to an end;

they are new every morning; great is your faithfulness.
—Lamentations 3:22-23

Page intentionally left blank.

...they who wait for the Lord
shall renew their strength;
they shall mount up with wings like eagles;
they shall run and not be weary;
they shall walk and not faint.
—Isaiah 40:31

Page intentionally left blank.

For I know the plans I have for you,
declares the Lord,
plans for welfare and not for evil,
to give you a future and a hope.
—Jeremiah 29:11

Page intentionally left blank.

And let us not grow weary of doing good,

for in due season we will reap, if we do not give up.
—Galatians 6:9

Page intentionally left blank.